Harcourt

NEXTGENERATION

read | talk | write

44Book™

Stage B

Printed in the U.S.A.

ISBN-13: 978-0-545-50124-8

2 3 4 5 6 7 8 9 10   8   24 23 22 21 20 19 18 17 16

4510000422

Table of Contents

Welcome to the *44Book* **6**

WORKSHOPS

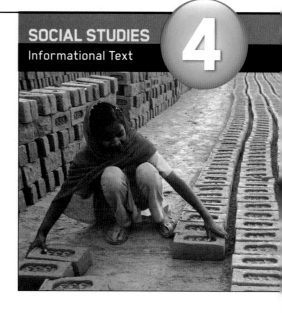
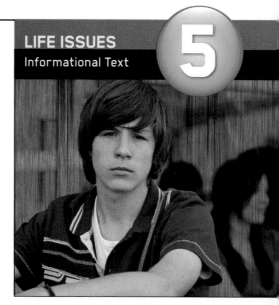

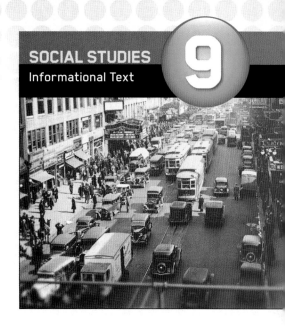

Welcome to the *44Book*

Get ready for the *44Book* by taking this quiz. After you finish each Workshop, check back to see if your ideas or opinions have changed.

START

1 Think about the Workshop title, "The New Americans." Look at the photo above. What do you predict this Workshop will be about? Explain your reasoning.

_____

_____

_____

_____

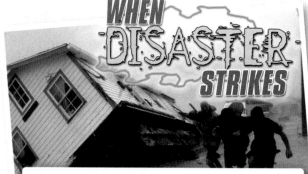

2 Read each statement. Write *A* if you agree. Write *D* if you disagree.

____ Volunteers can be helpful during disaster cleanup.

____ If a disaster is headed your way, you should leave your home and find shelter somewhere safer.

____ Once a disaster is over, the area it hit is no longer dangerous.

3 What determines people's identities? Check all that apply.

☐ their families   ☐ their cultures

☐ their choices   ☐ their possessions

☐ their homes

4 **Role-Play:** Look at the picture above. Then, imagine you have this girl's job. With a partner, take turns describing what a day in your life would be like.

5

Being a teen is tough. What puts the most pressure on teens? Rank these items.

1 = most pressure   4 = least pressure

_____ school   _____ family

_____ peers   _____ society

POE: The Master of Horror

6

What is the main reason why Edgar Allan Poe's stories are still read today?

____ They are assigned in schools.

____ Readers like their suspense and mystery.

____ People find new ways to tell them.

Alien INVADERS

7

Alien invaders like this bug can cause serious damage to the environment. Check the method you think is the best way to stop these invaders.

❑ with an invention that kills the invaders

❑ with special agents whose job is to keep the invaders from entering the country

THE STREETS OF HARLEM

9

Many cities are very different today than they were in the past. Read each statement. Write *A* if you agree. Write *D* if you disagree.

____ The most important parts of a city are the historical places that make it unique.

____ The most important parts of a city are the new, popular places for people to visit.

Turning Points

8

Can art help people face tough situations? Explain why or why not.

_____

_____

_____

FINISH

Workshops

The NEW Americans

How do immigrants' lives change in America?

The United States has always been a home for newcomers. Americans come from all over the world! Find out how their lives change here.

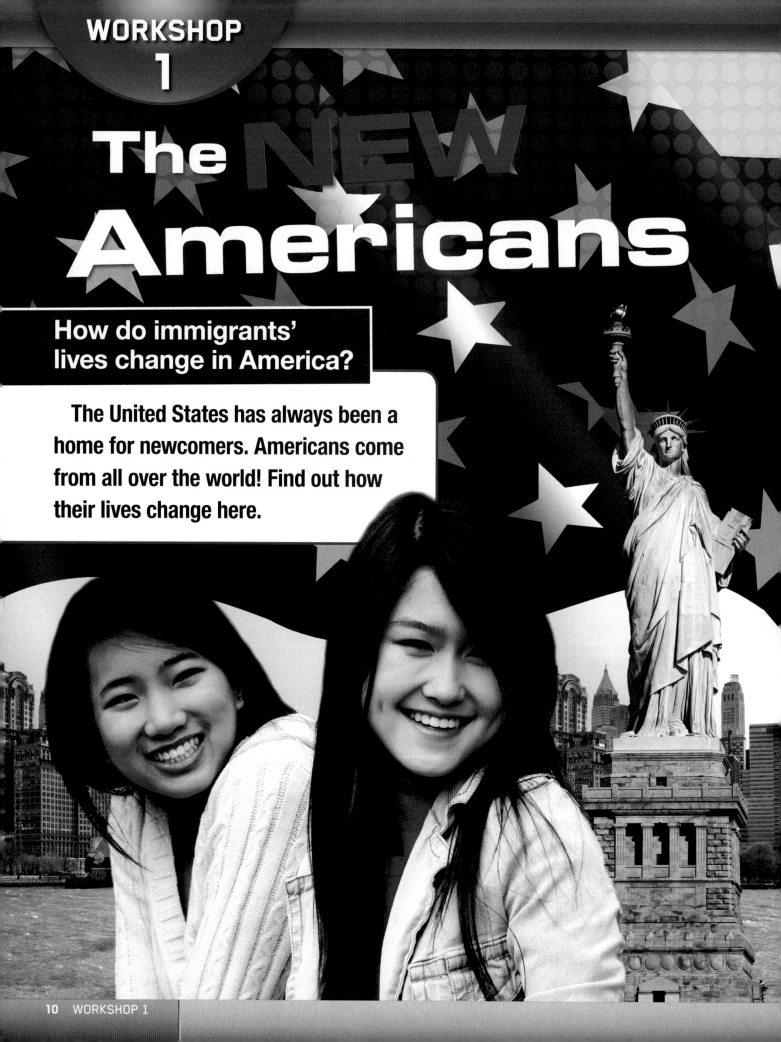

TEXT 1 Blog Post

Manzano Wins Medal

An Olympic runner wins a medal for his adopted country.

TEXT 2 Passport

Read Primary Sources

Analyze a passport from the past.

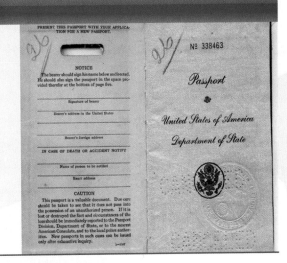

TEXT 3 News Article

Taking Sides

Not everyone agrees on how to help young immigrants.

Blending Sounds Into Words

Words are made up of individual **sounds**.

The single sounds are blended together to make a word.

These letters make the sounds /g/, /e/, /t/. Blended together, that's **get**.

Oh, I get it!

Blend It

Listen to the sound each letter stands for. Then blend the sounds together to make a word. Write the word on the line.

1. m a n _____

4. th e n _____

7. s t o ck _____

2. g o t _____

5. n e s t _____

8. s p i ll _____

3. n o d _____

6. t u s k _____

9. b l e n d _____

Picture Perfect

Listen to the sounds in each word. Blend the sounds together. Then write the word beside its picture.

1. sob

2. sun

3. jet

4. pin

5. neck

6. map

 _____

 _____

 _____

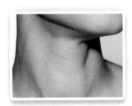 _____

 _____

 _____

Sentence Solver

Choose the correct words to complete the sentences.

1. We _____ use this _____ to cool the room. (fan, can)

2. It is too _____ to wear this _____ (hot, hat)

3. Please bring _____ my _____ (back, bag)

4. We _____ down the hill on a _____ (sled, slid)

TEXT 1
Blog Post

Main Idea and Details

1. ✔ Check the main idea.

2. ★ Star three important details.

3. What evidence from the text shows that Manzano is a hard worker?

   Manzano is a hard worker because _____

   _____

   _____

   _____

   _____

   _____

   _____

   _____

   _____

🔍 **Word Analysis**

Circle the S.M.A.R.T. words that begin and end with one consonant sound. Underline words that begin or end with two consonant sounds blended together.

Tyson's Olympic Updates

All you need to know about the 2012 Summer Games in London

TUESDAY, AUGUST 7, 2012

Manzano Wins Medal

Leo Manzano's hard work has paid off! He won the silver medal!

He ran in the 1,500 meter race. He came in second. He finished in 3 minutes and 34 seconds!

Manzano runs for the United States. He was born in Mexico. His family moved to Texas when he was four.

Manzano also works hard off the track. At age 11, he got his first job. He is the first in his family to graduate high school. He is also the first to go to college.

Congratulations to Leo! He has made the United States proud!

POSTED BY TYSON WALKER AT 4:25 PM

💬 Comment ✉ Share ★ Favorite

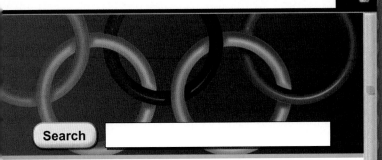

Search

ABOUT ME

My name is Tyson. I love the Olympics, especially the track and field events. I write all about them here on my blog.

RECENT POSTS

▶ FALL

▶ WINTER

▶ SPRING

▼ SUMMER

    ▶ June (10)

    ▶ July (18)

    ▼ August (8)

       Manzano Wins Medal

CONTACT

Email me here.

WORDS TO KNOW!

1,500 meters: a distance measurement equal to about .93 miles

track: a circular course around which people race

Word Count 96   Lexile 310L

Academic Discussion

Main Idea

Q: What is the main idea of the blog post?

A: The main idea of the blog post is _____.

Leo Manzano is an _____ who worked hard to win a medal at the 2012 Summer Olympics.

Important Details

Q: How is Leo Manzano a hard worker?

A: _____, Leo Manzano _____.

1. On the track:

2. Off the track:

Summarize

Describe Leo Manzano. Include the main idea and important details.

Read Primary Sources

Want to travel the world? Don't forget your passport! A passport is a **document**. It shows that the owner is a **citizen** of a certain country. **Immigrants** can get American passports when they become citizens. Below is a passport from the 1920s. What kind of information does it contain?

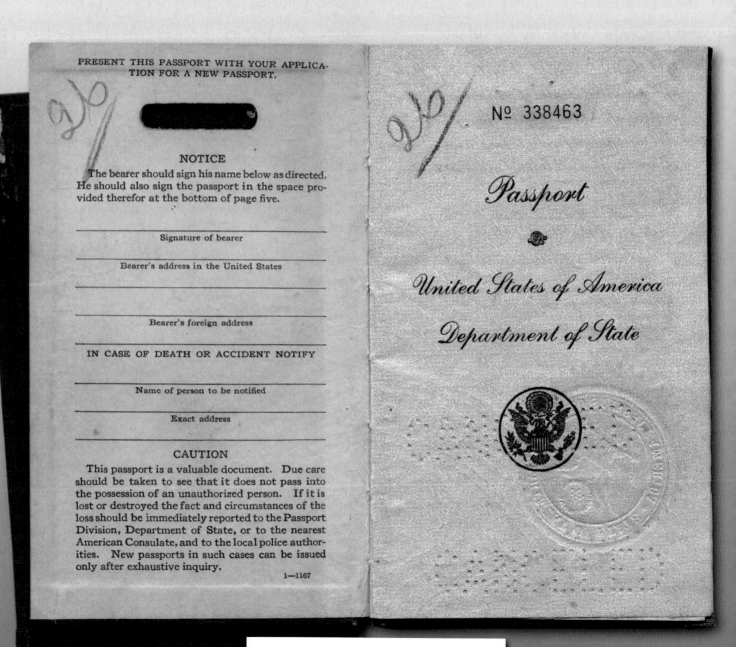

PRESENT THIS PASSPORT WITH YOUR APPLICATION FOR A NEW PASSPORT.

NOTICE

The bearer should sign his name below as directed. He should also sign the passport in the space provided therefor at the bottom of page five.

_____
Signature of bearer

_____
Bearer's address in the United States

_____
Bearer's foreign address

IN CASE OF DEATH OR ACCIDENT NOTIFY

_____
Name of person to be notified

_____
Exact address

CAUTION

This passport is a valuable document. Due care should be taken to see that it does not pass into the possession of an unauthorized person. If it is lost or destroyed the fact and circumstances of the loss should be immediately reported to the Passport Division, Department of State, or to the nearest American Consulate, and to the local police authorities. New passports in such cases can be issued only after exhaustive inquiry.

1—1167

Nº 338463

Passport

United States of America

Department of State

This passport is from the 1920s.

Build Word Knowledge

Target Word Read and rate each Target Word.*	Meaning Complete the Target Word meanings.
document *doc•u•ment* *(noun)* 1 2 3 4	official _____ that prove or support something
citizen *cit•i•zen* *(noun)* 1 2 3 4	a _____ who is legally a member of a country and has rights and responsibilities there

* Rating Scale

1 = I don't know it at all.	**3** = I think I know the word.
2 = I've seen it or heard it.	**4** = I know it and use it.

Analyze

Look at the passport to answer the questions below.

1. What are two pieces of information the bearer—the person this passport belongs to—had to write in the passport?

   The bearer had to write his or her _____

   _____

2. Why does the passport ask for the "signature of bearer"?

   Passports ask for the bearers' signatures _____

   _____

   _____

3. Why is a passport considered a "valuable document"?

   A passport is a valuable document because _____

   _____

   _____

Text-Based Questioning

Main Idea and Details

1. ✔ Check the topic of the debate.

2. ★ Star two important details.

3. What are people disagreeing about in this reading?

   People are disagreeing about whether or

   not _____

   _____

   _____

   _____

   _____

   _____

Word Analysis

Circle the S.M.A.R.T. words that begin and end with one consonant sound. Underline words that begin or end with two consonant sounds blended together.

Taking Sides

By CRYSTAL CARSON

Over 38 million immigrants live in the United States. Most are legal immigrants. They moved here with the government's permission.

Some immigrants came without permission. They currently do not have official documents saying they can live here. They are undocumented immigrants.

These young immigrants are caught in the middle.

Some of these immigrants are young people. They are the subjects of a debate. Should they be granted American citizenship? Some people think they should. Others do not.

For Citizenship

One side supports granting citizenship to some of these young immigrants. Their families brought them here when they were very young. Being undocumented was not their choice. If they are in college or the military, they should be allowed to apply for citizenship. Their hard work and ideas can have a positive influence on everyone.

Young people rallying to support citizenship for young undocumented immigrants.

Against Citizenship

Other people think **this** is wrong. These immigrants are here without permission, they say. It is unfair to grant them citizenship. Legal immigrants got permission. They did the right thing. They should become citizens first.

People continue to take sides in this debate. These young immigrants are caught in the middle.

WORDS TO KNOW!

permission: official approval to do something

grant: to give someone something they have asked for

Word Count **179**   Lexile **430L**

Academic Discussion

Main Idea

Q: What is the main idea of the article?

A: The main idea of the article is _____.

> People are debating whether or not young
>
> _____
>
> immigrants should become citizens.

Important Details

Q: What are the arguments that each side makes?

A: People who are _____ argue that _____.

1. For citizenship:

2. Against citizenship:

Summarize

Explain why some young immigrants are the subjects of a debate. Include the main idea and important details.

WHEN DISASTER STRIKES

How do we respond to the dark side of nature?

No matter where you live, natural disasters can find you. Storms can wreck entire towns! After a storm hits, it takes time and hard work to recover.

TEXT 1 Journal Entry

Storm Survivor

A young person recalls escaping a deadly hurricane in the Gulf of Mexico.

TEXT 2 Satellite Images

Read Primary Sources

Images from before and after a deadly tornado show its devastation.

TEXT 3 Brochure

Getting on the
Road to
Recovery

Find out tips for volunteer relief workers.

Segmenting Words Into Sounds

How do you spell your name?

It's J-O-N. Jon.

Jon

Segment, or break, a word into its sounds.

Blend the sounds together to read the word.

Count It

Read each word. Count the number of sounds in each word. Write the number on the line.

1. am _____

2. hat _____

3. it _____

4. trim _____

5. yes _____

6. back _____

Segment It

Break each word into its sounds. Write each sound in a box.

1. an ☐☐

2. sun ☐☐☐

3. pot ☐☐☐

4. went ☐☐☐☐

5. if ☐☐

6. shop ☐☐☐

Sort It

Write the words with two sounds and the words with three sounds in the correct box.

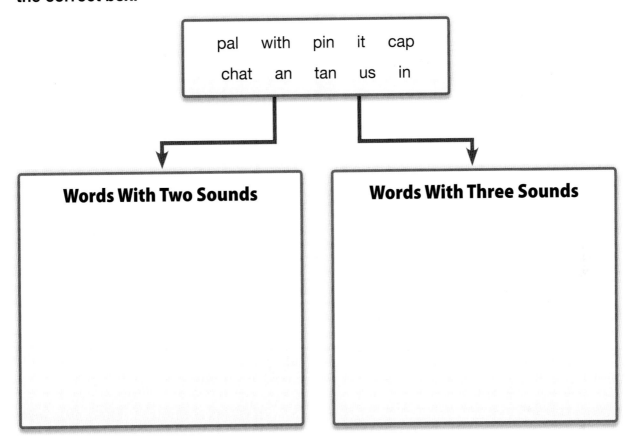

| pal | with | pin | it | cap |
| chat | an | tan | us | in |

Words With Two Sounds

Words With Three Sounds

Segment and Spell

Write the letters of the words you hear read aloud. Then write the word in the sentence.

1. _____ _____   I am _____ school.

2. _____ _____ _____   May I _____ your dog?

3. _____ _____ _____   A bug _____ me.

4. _____ _____ _____   I can _____ like a frog.

5. _____ _____ _____   We rode in a _____ to the game.

📖 Text-Based Questioning

Sequence of Events

1. Box the signal words that tell about sequence.

2. ★ Star three key events.

3. Tell what happened to Abigayle.

After two months, _____

_____

_____

Then, _____

_____

_____

Next, _____

_____

_____

After three years, _____

_____

_____

🔍 Word Analysis

Circle the S.M.A.R.T. words with three sounds. Underline the words with two sounds.

Storm Survivor

Abigayle Lista lives near New Orleans, Louisiana. She was nine years old when Hurricane Katrina hit in August 2005. She remembers what life was like after that terrible storm.

Monday, September 3

I remember evacuating. My parents and I stayed glued to TV news reports. We saw that my dad's office **was** damaged. We didn't know what had happened **to** our home.

After two months, the government let **us** return. Our house was flooded. It was covered in mold and mud.

Me!

Our house looked like this!

Then, my mom and I moved in with my grandparents. Next, my dad was transferred to Texas to work. After three years, we finally moved back home.

The **recovery** process has been difficult. But we will **not** be defeated. My family will stay strong.

Academic Discussion

Main Idea

Q: What is the main idea of the journal entry?

A: The main idea of the journal entry is _____.

Recovering from a hurricane is _____
_____

Important Details

Q: What happened to Abigayle after the hurricane?

A: _____ the hurricane, Abigayle _____.

1. Two months after:

2. Three years after:

Summarize

Explain what happened to Abigayle. Include the main idea and important details.

Read Primary Sources

It only took 38 minutes for life in Joplin, Missouri, to change completely. On May 22, 2011, a **major tornado** ripped through the town, lasting from 5:34 p.m. to 6:12 p.m. It killed over 150 people and injured 1,000. It also caused $2.8 billion in damage. Below are two **satellite** images of Joplin. The left side is Joplin before the tornado. The right side is after the tornado. What do these images show about the **destruction** that tornadoes cause?

Joplin High School

This image was taken in August, 2009, two years before the tornado.

This image was taken on May 24, 2011, two days after the tornado.

Build Word Knowledge

Target Word Read and rate each Target Word.*	Meaning Complete the Target Word meanings.
tornado *tor•na•do* *(noun)* 1 2 3 4	a violent wind storm with a funnel-shaped cloud that _____ very quickly and reaches down to the ground
satellite *sat•el•lite* *(noun)* 1 2 3 4	a machine that has been sent into _____ and travels around a planet, a moon, or the sun

* Rating Scale

1 = I don't know it at all.
2 = I've seen it or heard it.
3 = I think I know the word.
4 = I know it and use it.

Analyze

Use the images to complete the sentences below.

1. What are two features you notice in the image of Joplin before the tornado?

   Two features I notice are _____

   _____

2. How have these features changed in the image after the tornado?

   After the tornado, _____

   _____

   _____

3. Why are satellite images helpful in surveying damage from a storm?

   Satellite images are helpful because _____

   _____

   _____

Text-Based Questioning

Sequence of Events

1. ✔ Check the signal words or phrases that tell about the sequence of events.

2. Tell about the steps that relief workers should follow.

First, volunteers should _____

_____

_____

After authorities say it is safe, volunteers

should _____

_____

_____

_____

Next, they should _____

_____

_____

_____

Finally, after following these steps, they

_____

_____

_____

_____

Word Analysis

(Circle) the S.M.A.R.T. words with three sounds. Underline the words with two sounds.

Getting on the Road to Recovery

Volunteer relief workers should follow these steps to clean up after a disaster.

1 First, find gear that will protect you while you work. You will need a hard hat, work gloves, heavy boots, and earplugs.

2 After authorities say it is **safe**, go to the area you will be cleaning. Find the other volunteers. You will be working as a team to clean up the area.

3 Next, make a plan. Decide what each team member will **do**. Set clear goals. Break large jobs into smaller parts.

4 Finally, you are ready to begin the cleanup. Be careful moving objects. To **prevent** injuries, **use** teams of two or more people to lift heavy objects.

In hot weather, drink plenty of water. Take breaks in cool places. Work outdoors when it is cooler.

Leave right away if you hear an unusual noise or smell gas. Tell authorities. Then, wait for their permission to return.

Wash with soap and water after you stop working.

WORDS TO KNOW!

relief: help; assistance

authorities: people in charge

Word Count **146**   Lexile **490L**

Academic Discussion

Main Idea

Q: What is the main idea of the brochure?

A: The main idea of the brochure is _____.

Relief workers should follow _____

_____ when they

prepare to clean up after a disaster.

Important Details

Q: What tips should you follow when you clean up after a disaster?

A: If you are _____, you should _____.

1. Moving objects:

2. In hot weather:

Summarize

Explain how volunteer relief workers should help clean up after a disaster. Include the main idea and important details.

Identity *Crisis*

What makes you who you are?

What defines who you are? Is it where you are from? Is it your family? Or is it something else?

TEXT 1   Magazine Article

Place and Personality

Research shows that where you live could be a clue to who you are.

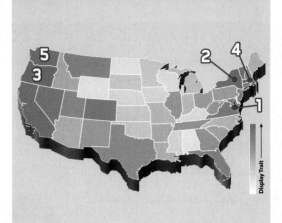

TEXT 2   Poem & Painting

Read Primary Sources

Analyze a poem and painting about a life-changing journey.

TEXT 3   Personal Essay

THIS LAND IS MY LAND?

Read a young woman's award-winning essay about her culture.

Contrasting Long and Short Vowels

Short vowel sounds are the sounds you hear in the middle of *hat*, *hem*, *hit*, *hop*, and *hum*.

Long vowel sounds are the same as the letters' names in the alphabet.

Long Vowel Sounds

Write the letter of the long vowel sound you hear read aloud.

1. s ☐ m e
2. ☐ v e
3. m ☐ n e
4. h ☐ m e
5. m ☐ t e
6. ☐ c e

Short Vowel Sounds

Write the letter of the short vowel sound you hear read aloud.

1. b ☐ t
2. l ☐ d
3. h ☐ t
4. l ☐ t
5. r ☐ n
6. ☐ t

Long and Short Vowel Sounds

Ⓒircle the words with short vowel sounds. <u>Underline</u> the words with long vowel sounds.

hid	hide	cod	code
huge	hug	mad	made

Practice

Write the short and long vowel words in the correct box.

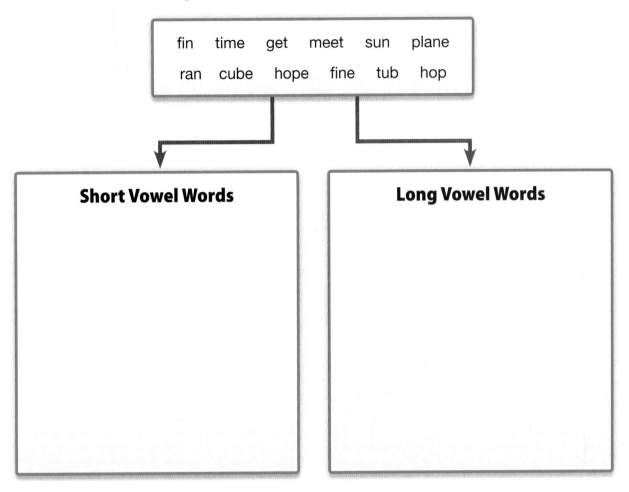

| fin | time | get | meet | sun | plane |
| ran | cube | hope | fine | tub | hop |

Short Vowel Words

Long Vowel Words

Context Clues

Write the correct word in the blank.

1. I _____ an apple. (at, ate)

2. I stayed _____ my cousin's house. (at, ate)

3. I had a _____ in my jeans. (rip, ripe)

4. The fruit was _____ (rip, ripe)

5. I took a bath in the _____ (tub, tube)

6. Air moved through the _____ (tub, tube)

Text-Based Questioning

Make Inferences

1. Why did researchers poll "more than 600,000 Americans"?

   Researchers polled them to find out _____

   _____

   _____

2. Why did Dr. Rentfrow call his study *The Geography of Personality*?

   Dr. Rentfrow called his study this because

   _____

   _____

   _____

Vocabulary & Language

3. Based on the context clues in paragraph 5, what does the word *accepting* mean?

   The word *accepting* means to treat

   someone or something with _____

   _____

Word Analysis

Circle the S.M.A.R.T. words with a short vowel sound. Underline the words with a long vowel sound.

Place and Personality

by Isaac Seidel

Scientists find a link between where you live and what you are like.

Is where you live a clue to your **identity**? Dr. Jason Rentfrow says yes!

Dr. Rentfrow and his team of researchers spent six years collecting research for their study, *The Geography of Personality*.

They polled more than 600,000 Americans. They asked them questions. The way people **responded** depended on their personalities. The researchers analyzed the answers. They noticed trends in people's personalities based on where they lived.

The researchers found that people from the South and Midwest are the most agreeable. They are easygoing. Residents of these states also tend to be friendlier.

People from the Northeast and the West Coast are the most open-minded. They are more accepting of different people and ideas.

Not everyone in a state has the same personality. But this study shows definite personality patterns. Does your personality fit the trends?

Trait: Open-Mindedness

This map shows the researchers' findings for one of the personality traits they studied: open-mindedness. The darkened states have high numbers of open-minded people living there.

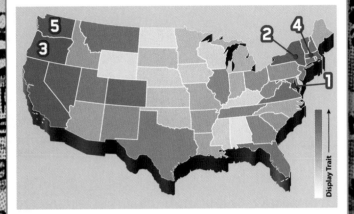

Display Trait

Top 5 Most Open-Minded Places:

1. Washington, D.C.
2. New York
3. Oregon
4. Massachusetts
5. Washington State

Word Count 136   Lexile 590L

Academic Discussion

Main Idea

Q: What is the main idea of the article?

A: The main idea of the article is _____.

> Researchers found a link between where
>
> people live and _____

Important Details

Q: What did researchers find out about the personalities of people in different states?

A: People who _____ are more likely to _____.

> **1.** Live in the South and Midwest:
>
>
>
>
>
> **2.** Live in the Northeast and on the West Coast:

Summarize

Explain what researchers found out about states and personalities. Include the main idea and important details.

Read Primary Sources

A journey to a new place can transform someone forever. Read this poem and study the painting. The **speaker** in the poem and the **subject** of the painting leave their homes behind for somewhere new. How does this change their identities?

Epilogue

by Grace Nichols

I have crossed an ocean
I have lost my tongue
from the root of the old
one
a new one has sprung

This painting was done by artist Paula Nicho Cumez. She is from Guatemala, a country in Central America.

Build Word Knowledge

Target Word Read and rate each Target Word.*	Meaning Complete the Target Word meanings.
speaker speak•er (noun) 1 2 3 4	someone who _____ something
subject sub•ject (noun) 1 2 3 4	the thing or _____ that is the main focus of a work of art

* Rating Scale   1 = I don't know it at all.   3 = I think I know the word.
                      2 = I've seen it or heard it.   4 = I know it and use it.

Analyze

Use the poem and painting to answer the questions below.

1. What does the phrase "crossed an ocean" mean?

It means that the speaker in the poem has _____

_____

2. What does it mean that the speaker has lost her "tongue"?

She has crossed an ocean, so she now has to _____

_____

3. The painting shows a woman flying away. How does the painting illustrate the poem?

The painting illustrates the poem because _____

_____

_____

📖 Text-Based Questioning

Make Inferences

1. What does Tasnim mean when she says, "I never found the home where I belong"?

   Tasnim means that she never _____

   _____

   _____

   _____

2. What parts of her Egyptian heritage helped Tasnim establish her identity?

   Tasnim learned more about _____

   _____

   _____

   _____

   _____

Vocabulary & Language

3. What is a synonym for the word *grasped* in paragraph 1?

   A synonym for *grasped* is _____

   _____

🔍 Word Analysis

Circle the S.M.A.R.T. words with a short vowel sound. Underline the words with a long vowel sound.

THIS LAND IS MY LAND?

Tasnim Mohamed grew up in Texas. Her family moved to America from Egypt when she was very young. When she was in high school, Tasnim started learning about her Egyptian heritage. This helped her discover her **unique** identity. She wrote about this experience in this personal essay, which won a Scholastic Writing Award.

I grasped the American culture quicker than anyone else in my family. It was the only culture to which I was exposed.

I have lived in America for fifteen years now. I have lived in a state and a country. I have lived in a city and a house. But I never found the home where I belong.

But now I realize who I am. I feel pride in my [Egyptian] culture. I am learning more about my faith and my language. I am learning more about my culture and my country.

Any land can be my land as long as I continue to be who I am. Where I live versus where I was born does not matter. What matters is who I am as a person.

WORDS TO KNOW!

exposed: having experienced new ideas or ways of life

versus: as opposed to

Word Count 181   Lexile 520L

Academic Discussion

Main Idea

Q: What is the main idea of the essay?

A: The main idea of the essay is _____.

Tasnim learned that where she lives or where she is from is not as important as

_____

_____

Important Details

Q: How did Tasnim feel before and after she started to learn about her Egyptian culture?

A: _____ Tasnim started learning about her culture, she _____.

1. Before:

2. After:

Summarize

Explain how Tasnim discovered who she was as a person. Include the main idea and important details.

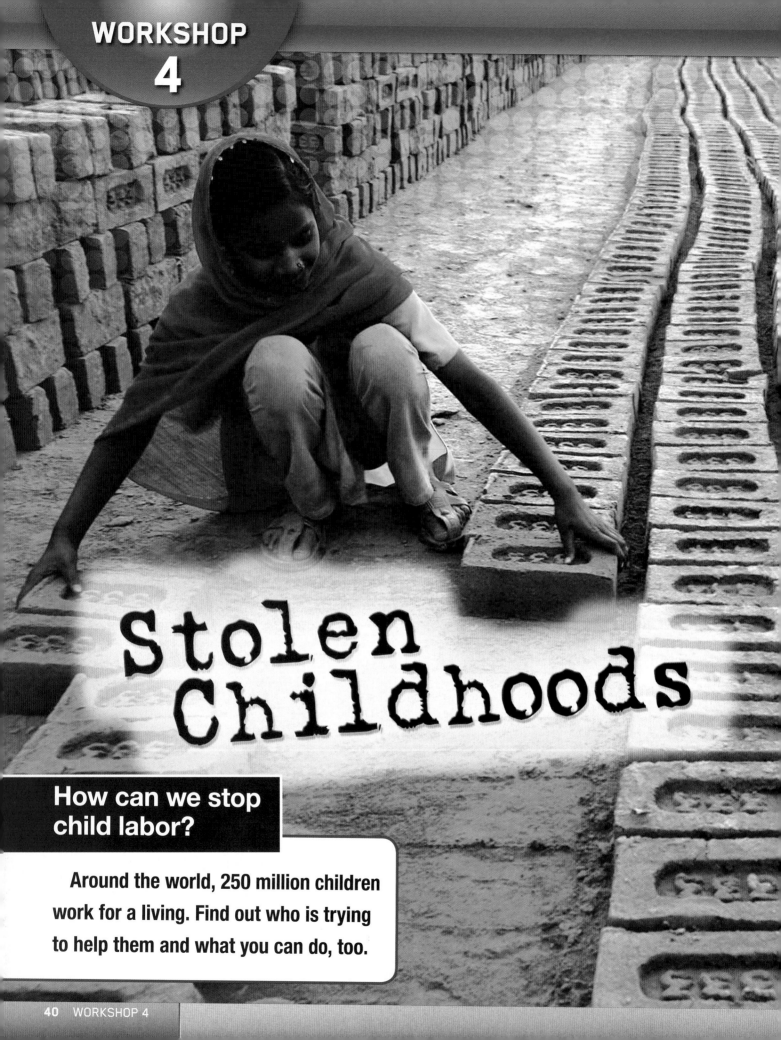

Stolen Childhoods

How can we stop child labor?

Around the world, 250 million children work for a living. Find out who is trying to help them and what you can do, too.

TEXT 1 Web Page

Iqbal's Legacy

A charity Iqbal inspired continues his fight today.

TEXT 2 Editorial Cartoon

Read Primary Sources

An editorial cartoon can make a statement that speaks louder than words.

TEXT 3 Magazine Article

YOU CAN HELP END

CHILD LABOR

Can you fight child labor without ever leaving home?

Recognizing and Using Contractions

Do not bother John's **dog. It is asleep.**

Don't bother Lisa's **cat. It's asleep, too.**

A **contraction** is formed by combining two words, with some letters left out. An apostrophe takes the place of the missing letters.

An apostrophe can also show possession. Do not confuse **possessives** with contractions.

Match It

Match each contraction with its word pair.

| won't | didn't | he's | they'll | wasn't |

1. he is _____

2. they will _____

3. was not _____

4. did not _____

5. will not _____

Write It

Read each contraction. Write the words that form the contraction.

1. hadn't _____

2. it's _____

3. doesn't _____

4. she's _____

5. they've _____

6. aren't _____

7. we'll _____

8. don't _____

9. they're _____

10. we're _____

Analyze Words

Circle each word with an apostrophe. Write *P* if it is a possessive and *C* if it is a contraction.

1. We haven't eaten dinner yet. _____

2. I lost my friend's computer. _____

3. You can't swim during a storm. _____

4. She's home sick today. _____

5. Our school's band won the contest. _____

6. I don't want to see that movie. _____

Use Contractions

Write a contraction in the blank to complete the sentences.

1. I _____ spread rumors. (will not)

2. _____ be here soon. (she will)

3. _____ go to the park. (let us)

4. I think _____ going on a trip. (he is)

5. I _____ know the answer. (do not)

6. _____ your brother? (Where is)

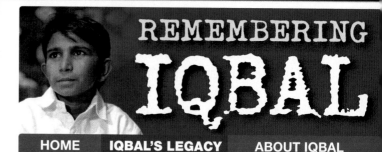

Text-Based Questioning

Summarize

1. What is the topic of the first two paragraphs?

   The topic of the first two paragraphs is

   that Craig's and Iqbal's lives _____

   _____

   _____

2. <u>Underline</u> two details in the first two paragraphs that tell more about the topic.

3. Summarize the first two paragraphs in your own words with a partner.

Vocabulary & Language

4. How does the suffix -*less* change the meaning of *power* in the word *powerless* in paragraph 4?

   Adding -*less* to the word *power* changes

   the word to mean _____

   _____

Word Analysis

(Circle) the S.M.A.R.T. words that are contractions. Tell a partner what two words make up each contraction.

REMEMBERING IQBAL

HOME   IQBAL'S LEGACY   ABOUT IQBAL

Iqbal's Legacy

Craig Kielburger was twelve years old when he read about Iqbal Masih. Both boys were the same age. But their lives **weren't** similar at all.

Craig went to school. Iqbal **didn't**. He went to work. While Craig played with friends, Iqbal was forced to weave carpets for long hours.

Craig read about how Iqbal had escaped the carpet factory and started fighting child **labor** practices. He also read that Iqbal was killed. Iqbal's bravery inspired Craig. He decided to take action.

Craig started a charity called Free the Children. The organization raises money to end poverty and exploitation for powerless children around the world.

Free the Children teaches young people. They learn how they can help other young people on an **international** level. So far, **they've** made a big difference. Free the Children has built schools. It has given

A site dedicated to Iqbal Masih and his fight against child labor

Search ▶

IQBAL IN THE MEDIA　　　**LINKS**　　　**CONTACT**

people food and water. It has helped people get medical care. And, of course, it has fought against child labor.

Iqbal died young. But Free the Children makes sure that his mission **isn't** forgotten.

Schools funded by Free the Children educate 55,000 students daily.

WORDS TO KNOW!

practices: things that people do often and in a particular way

exploitation: a situation where someone is unfairly asked to do something for little in return

Word Count **173**　　Lexile **510L**

Academic Discussion

Main Idea

Q: What is the main idea of the web page?

A: The main idea of the web page is _____.

> Iqbal Masih inspired Craig Kielburger to
>
> _____
>
> that _____

Important Details

Q: What are the goals and accomplishments of Free the Children?

A: The _____ of Free the Children _____.

> 1. Goals:
>
>
>
> 2. Accomplishments:

Summarize

Explain how Free the Children began and how it helps children worldwide. Include the main idea and important details.

Read Primary Sources

Some people say a picture is worth a thousand words. **Editorial** cartoonists might agree with them! Cartoonists use drawings to express their opinions on issues of the day. This editorial cartoon by Robert Minor appeared in *The Daily Worker* on December 22, 1924. What was Minor trying to say about child labor?

Build Word Knowledge

Target Word Read and rate each Target Word.*	Meaning Complete the Target Word meanings.
editorial ed•i•to•ri•al (noun) [1] [2] [3] [4]	a drawing or piece of writing that gives the author's _____ about something
criticize crit•i•cize (verb) [1] [2] [3] [4]	to _____ disapproval in someone or something, or to talk about _____

* Rating Scale	**1** = I don't know it at all. **2** = I've seen it or heard it.	**3** = I think I know the word. **4** = I know it and use it.

Analyze

Look at the editorial cartoon to answer the questions below.

1. How does the artist show that the man in the cartoon is a powerful businessman?

The artist drew the man _____

to show that he is a powerful businessman.

2. What is the man doing in the cartoon?

The man is _____

3. Why did the artist choose to draw the children so much smaller than the man?

The artist drew the children so small to show _____

_____

4. How does this editorial cartoon criticize businesspeople who use child labor?

The artist is saying that businesspeople who use child labor are _____

because _____

_____

Text-Based Questioning

Summarize

1. What is the topic of the paragraph titled "Get the Facts"?

   Learn which companies _____

   _____

   _____

2. <u>Underline</u> two details in the paragraph titled "Get the Facts" that tell about the topic.

3. Summarize the second paragraph in your own words to a partner.

Vocabulary & Language

4. What does the word *reform* mean in the introduction?

   The word *reform* means to _____

   _____

   something so that it operates in a fairer way.

Word Analysis

(Circle) the S.M.A.R.T. words that are contractions. Tell a partner what two words make up each contraction.

YOU CAN HELP END CHILD LABOR

by Didi Jackson

Every day, millions of children are forced to work for long hours and little pay. But you can help. Follow these steps to help reform child labor.

1 Get the Facts

Do you know who made your sneakers? What about your soccer ball? Go online to find out where the products you buy are made. Learn which companies **don't** use child labor. Look for companies that protect the rights of workers. Find out who's paying their adult workers enough money for them to have what they need. When adults earn enough money to live on, their children **benefit**. They don't have to work, too.

2 Use Your Buying Power

Let your money do the talking. Talk to store owners. Share what you know about child labor. Tell them **you'll** only buy products **produced** without child labor.

These labels mean the products were made without child labor.

3 Write to Fight

You've got power in your words. Write letters to politicians. Ask them to support children's rights abroad. Tell them that children need a safe, healthy place to grow.

4 Take Action

Join a group at school that fights child labor practices. **Can't** find one? Start your own! Groups have strength in numbers. They raise money and organize protests. They can help, and so can you.

WORDS TO KNOW!

abroad: in another country

protest: planned gatherings where groups of people stand up for a cause

Word Count 201   Lexile 470L

Academic Discussion

Main Idea

Q: What is the main idea of the article?

A: The main idea of the article is _____.

There are _____ you can take to help end _____ _____

Important Details

Q: What can you do to fight child labor?

A: When you _____, you should _____.

1. Get the facts:

2. Write to fight:

3. Take action:

Summarize

Explain what you can do to help stop child labor practices. Include the main idea and important details.

Writing Text Type

Informational Summary

An **informational summary** provides an overview of key topics and ideas from a text.

Read Diamond Johnson's informational summary of "Working in the Fields."

Topic Sentence

The **topic sentence** identifies the title, author, and text type the writer will summarize.

1. **UNDERLINE** the topic sentence.
2. **BOX** the controlling idea.

Detail Sentences

Details from the summarized text support the topic sentence with relevant facts, examples, and data.

3. ✔ **CHECK** three relevant details.

Language Use

Transition words and phrases introduce and connect ideas.

4. **CIRCLE** four transition words or phrases.

Citations from the text appear in quotation marks, with the page number in parentheses.

5. **DOUBLE UNDERLINE** two citations.

Concluding Sentence

The **concluding sentence** restates the controlling idea from the topic sentence and adds a final thought.

6. ★ **STAR** the concluding sentence.

Student Model

A Difficult Life
by Diamond Johnson

The magazine article "Working in the Fields," by Lee Rosenberg, discusses the hard lives of teen migrant workers. According to Rosenberg, teen migrant workers "sacrifice their time and freedom" to help their families (94). Unlike other teens, these workers don't lead carefree lives full of school and friends. Instead, they work long hours in the hot sun for low wages. In addition, most of them come from other countries, often illegally. They use the money they earn to help their families. Though their lives are difficult, some teen workers look to improve their circumstances. As Rodrigo, a teen migrant worker who takes night classes, says, "I want a better life" (96). In summary, teen migrant workers lead hard lives, but some of them hold out hope for a better future.

P 1

Brainstorm

Read the writing prompt. Then use the boxes to brainstorm ideas.

Important Idea	Details to Support This Idea

Writing Prompt:
Write a paragraph summarizing
"Child Labor Around the World."

Important Idea	Details to Support This Idea

Choose Your Topic

Use ideas and details from your idea web to help you state your topic.

I plan to summarize the social studies text _____

This text discusses the topic of _____

_____

Organize Ideas for Writing

Complete this outline with notes for your informational summary.

    I. Topic Sentence. Identify the text and include a controlling idea.

      Topic: _____

      Controlling Idea: _____

    II. Detail Sentences. List two details that support the topic sentence.

      Detail 1: _____

      Detail 2: _____

    III. Concluding Sentence. Restate the main idea and add a final thought.

      _____

      _____

Write Your First Draft

Write your topic sentence.

WORD CHOICES	
Everyday	**Precise**
work	toil
stop	ban, prevent
pay	income, wages

Topic Sentence

The social studies text "Child Labor Around the World," by

_____, is about _____
       (author)   (topic)

_____ .

Type your topic sentence on the computer or write it on paper. Then use these transition words and phrases to complete a draft of your summary.

Detail Sentences

The text begins, . . .	*For instance, . . .*
In addition, . . .	*It also notes that, . . .*

Concluding Sentence

In conclusion . . .	*Overall . . .*	*To sum up . . .*

Revise Your Paragraph

Evaluate: Rate your summary paragraph. Then have a writing partner rate it.

Scoring Guide			
needs improvement	average	good	excellent
1	2	3	4

1. **UNDERLINE** the topic sentence. Does it state the title, author, and text type being summarized?

   Self   1   2   3   4

   Partner 1   2   3   4

2. **BOX** the controlling idea. Does it make a point about the text?

   Self   1   2   3   4

   Partner 1   2   3   4

3. ✔**CHECK** the details. Do relevant details support the topic sentence?

   Self   1   2   3   4

   Partner 1   2   3   4

4. **CIRCLE** transition words and phrases. Do they connect ideas?

   Self   1   2   3   4

   Partner 1   2   3   4

5. **DOUBLE UNDERLINE** citations. Does the page number appear in parentheses?

   Self   1   2   3   4

   Partner 1   2   3   4

6. ★**STAR** the concluding sentence. Does it restate the controlling idea and add a final thought?

   Self   1   2   3   4

   Partner 1   2   3   4

Discuss: Give feedback on your partner's informational summary.

1. Start with a positive comment about your partner's informational summary.

   The strongest part of your summary is

   _____

   _____ .

2. Give your partner suggestions for revision.

   You need more details about _____

   _____

   _____ .

   Your summary needs to include _____

   _____

   _____ .

3. Answer any questions your partner has about your suggestions.

4. Ask your partner for feedback. Use the frames below to summarize your partner's feedback.

   The strongest part of my summary is . . .

   I need more details about . . .

   My summary needs to include . . .

Revise Now, revise your informational summary.

UNDER PRESSURE

How do we handle pressure?

Being a teenager is tough. Teens are under serious pressure. When do people stand up to pressure? When do they give in?

TEXT 1 News Article

Science Whiz Succeeds

A high-school senior stays strong despite outside obstacles.

TEXT 2 Photograph

Read Primary Sources

An image captures someone who stood up to pressure—and others who did not.

TEXT 3 Encyclopedia Entry

The Third Wave

A teacher's lesson shows the dangers of being a follower.

Understanding Syllables

Cool!

A long word is easier to read if you split it into syllables.

A **syllable** has only one vowel sound—called a **vowel spot**. A vowel spot may be spelled with more than one vowel.

Groov / y!

Fan / tas / tic!

Identify Vowel Spots

Read each word. <u>Underline</u> each vowel spot in the word.

1. truck

2. limitless

3. robin

4. happen

5. plastic

6. habit

7. handful

8. cabinet

9. mess

10. dust

11. talentless

12. bonds

created strict rules, membership cards, a motto, and even a special greeting only for members. The Third Wave was not real. But the students thought it was.

At first, things went well. The class was well-behaved. They liked The Third Wave. They felt they belonged to a special group.

Soon, the students' behavior became alarming. The Third Wave grew from 30 students to over 200. Students dressed in identical white shirts. The Third Wave was all they talked about. They reported anyone who **rebelled**, and they looked down on nonmembers.

The Ending

After just one week, Jones ended the experiment. He revealed the truth: The Third Wave did not exist. Students were shocked. They were also embarrassed. In just a few days, they had become mindless followers. They finally understood Jones's lesson.

WORDS TO KNOW!

dictatorships: countries ruled by a person with complete power

movement: a group of people who have the same beliefs or goals

Word Count **221** Lexile **530L**

Main Idea

Q: What is the main idea of the entry?

A: The main idea of the entry is _____.

The Third Wave taught students why

people _____

_____

Important Details

Q: How did Ron Jones teach this lesson?

A: To make students _____, Jones _____.

1. Understand dictatorships:

2. Follow The Third Wave:

3. Stop their alarming behavior:

Summarize

Explain the purpose of The Third Wave. Include the main idea and important details.

Writing Text Type

Argument Paragraph

An **argument** states a position or claim about an issue. The writer supports the claim with convincing evidence and reasons.

Read Derek White's argument about a serious problem teenagers face today.

Topic Sentence

The **topic sentence** introduces the issue.

1. **UNDERLINE** the topic sentence.

The topic sentence also presents the writer's **claim,** or position, about the issue.

2. **BOX** the claim.

Detail Sentences

Convincing reasons and relevant evidence support the claim.

3. ✔ **CHECK** three reasons or pieces of evidence.

A strong argument points out weaknesses in **opposing arguments.**

4. → **PUT AN ARROW** next to an opposing argument.

Language Use

Transition words and phrases introduce and connect ideas in the paragraph.

5. **CIRCLE** two transition words or phrases.

Concluding Sentence

The **concluding sentence** restates the claim and offers a recommendation to the reader.

6. ★ **STAR** the concluding sentence.

Student Model

Bullying Is Bad
by Derek White

I think that bullying is the worst problem teenagers face today. Bullying comes in many forms. One is physical bullying. Another is verbal bullying, such as name-calling. A third and newer form of bullying is cyber-bullying, or bullying over the Internet. Regardless of the type, bullying is hurtful and can even ruin lives. Teens who are bullied in school may drop out or become bad students. Teens who are cyber-bullied may lose their self-confidence. Some people believe that bullying is not a serious problem. However, the statistics prove them wrong. Almost one-third of today's teens have been involved in some kind of bullying. That number proves this is a major issue. Therefore, I recommend that parents, teachers, and even teens themselves take a tougher stance against bullying and help put a stop to this hurtful problem.

Brainstorm

Read the writing prompt. Then use the boxes to help you brainstorm ideas.

Problems With Friendships

Problems in School

Writing Prompt:
Write an argument paragraph about the most serious problem teenagers face today. Support your argument with evidence from the Workshop readings.

Problems With Self-Esteem

Problems Outside of School

State Your Position

Use ideas from your idea web to help you determine your position. Then complete the sentences.

I will argue that the most serious problem teens face is _____

because _____

_____

Organize Ideas for Writing

Complete this outline with notes for your argument paragraph.

    I. Topic Sentence. Present the issue and your claim about it.

        Issue: _____

        Claim: _____

    II. Detail Sentences. List reasons or evidence to support your claim.

        Detail 1: _____

        Detail 2: _____

    III. Concluding Sentence. Restate your claim and make a recommendation.

        In summary, _____

        _____

Write Your First Draft

Write your topic sentence.

WORD CHOICES	
Everyday	**Precise**
bad	dreadful, terrible
problem	challenge
risk	hazard, threat

Topic Sentence

The worst problem teenagers face today is _____
(topic)

because _____
(claim)

_____

Type your topic sentence on the computer or write it on paper. Then use some of these transition words and phrases to complete a draft of your paragraph.

Detail Sentences

First of all, . . .	*For instance, . . .*
The most important reason . . .	*Though some people claim that . . .*

Concluding Sentence

In summary, . . .	*It is important to . . .*

Revise Your Paragraph

Evaluate: Rate your argument paragraph. Then have a writing partner rate it.

Scoring Guide			
needs improvement	average	good	excellent
1	2	3	4

1. **UNDERLINE** the topic sentence. Does it introduce the issue clearly?
   - Self   1   2   3   4
   - Partner 1   2   3   4

2. **BOX** the claim. Does it express the writer's position on the issue?
   - Self   1   2   3   4
   - Partner 1   2   3   4

3. ✔**CHECK** the reasons and evidence. Are they convincing and relevant?
   - Self   1   2   3   4
   - Partner 1   2   3   4

4. → **PUT AN ARROW** next to an opposing argument. Does the paragraph point out a weakness?
   - Self   1   2   3   4
   - Partner 1   2   3   4

5. **CIRCLE** transition words and phrases. Do they connect ideas?
   - Self   1   2   3   4
   - Partner 1   2   3   4

6. ★ **STAR** the conclusion. Does it offer a recommendation?
   - Self   1   2   3   4
   - Partner 1   2   3   4

Discuss: Give feedback on your partner's argument paragraph.

1. Start with a positive comment about your partner's argument paragraph.

   You did an effective job of _____

   _____

   _____

2. Give your partner suggestions for revision.

   Your claim would be stronger if you

   _____

   _____

   _____

   To support this point better, you could

   _____

   _____

   _____

3. Answer any questions your partner has about your suggestions.

4. Ask your partner for feedback. Use the frames below to summarize your partner's feedback.

   I did an effective job of . . .
   A strong part of my argument is . . .
   You had a question about . . .
   Two changes I need to make are . . .

> **Revise** Now, revise your argument paragraph.

POE:
The Master of Horror

Why do we tell Poe's stories today?

Edgar Allan Poe's creepy stories terrified the people of his time. His work still thrills readers today. Writers and artists find new ways to retell his scary tales.

TEXT 1 Blog Post

The Mystery of Poe's Birthday Visitor

A real-life mystery involving Poe's grave has puzzled people for decades.

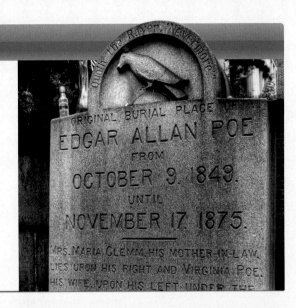

TEXT 2 Caricature

Read Primary Sources

Caricatures capture famous people in amusing and interesting ways.

TEXT 3 Graphic Novel

THE PREMATURE BURIAL

A graphic novelist uses a modern style to tell one of Poe's classic stories.

Unlocking Multisyllable Words

I am **unlocking** this door.

I am **un-lock-ing** this word!

Long words are easier to read if you split them into parts. You can add word parts to **base words**.

Prefixes are word parts added to the beginning of base words to change their meaning.

Suffixes and **endings** are word parts added to the end of base words to change their meaning or part of speech.

Identify Base Words

Read each word. Then circle its base word.

1. handed
2. frosting
3. unlimited
4. defrost

5. unpack
6. limitless
7. defrosted
8. locked

9. unlock
10. unwell
11. packing
12. wellness

13. limited
14. handful
15. unlocking
16. unpacked

Analyze Word Parts

Complete the chart by breaking each word into parts. Some words may not have a prefix or a suffix/ending.

	Prefix	Base Word	Suffix/Ending
1. nonfiction	non	fiction	
2. preheating			
3. dislikable			
4. narrowest			
5. overcrowded			
6. unpack			
7. agreeable			
8. incorrectly			

Determine Meaning

Read each clue below. Then add a prefix, suffix, and/or ending to each base word to form a word that matches the clue.

de-   non-   un-   -ed   -ful   -ing   -ness

1. without fat: _____ fat _____

2. the state of being late: _____ late _____

3. getting rid of frost: _____ frost _____

4. full of hope: _____ hope _____

5. without limits: _____ limit _____

TEXT 1
Blog Post

📖 Text-Based Questioning

Make Inferences

1. How do you think Poe's birthday visitor felt about Poe?

   I think Poe's birthday visitor _____

   _____

   _____

   _____

2. What evidence from the text makes you think this?

   I think this because _____

   _____

   _____

   _____

Vocabulary & Language

3. What does the prefix *re-* mean?

   The prefix *re-* means _____

4. At the end of paragraph 6, how does adding the prefix *re-* change the meaning of the word *appear*?

   The prefix *re-* changes the word to mean

   _____

🔍 Word Analysis

(Circle) the S.M.A.R.T. words with a prefix. Underline the S.M.A.R.T. words with a suffix. Then, divide each S.M.A.R.T. word into syllables.

---

http://www.blogplace.com/new

House of Horror
A BLOG FOR FANS OF SPOOKY STORIES

SATURDAY, JANUARY 19

The Mystery of Poe's Birthday Visitor

ORIGINAL BURIAL PLACE OF
EDGAR ALLAN POE
FROM
OCTOBER 9, 1849.
UNTIL
NOVEMBER 17, 1875.

MRS. MARIA CLEMM, HIS MOTHER-IN-LAW,
LIES UPON HIS RIGHT AND VIRGINIA POE,
HIS WIFE, UPON HIS LEFT, UNDER THE
MONUMENT ERECTED TO HIM IN THIS
CEMETERY.

A shadowy figure slipped quietly into the Westminster Burying Ground in Baltimore, Maryland. A large black hat hid his face. He approached a grave and laid three red roses on it. Then, he disappeared into the night.

While this situation sounds like a story by Edgar Allan Poe, it is not fiction. It is a real-life mystery that has puzzled **generations** of people for 60 years.

Search

Although this is not a story Poe wrote, he is still part of the mystery. The grave the unknown figure visited is Poe's. And the visits occurred every January 19, the date of the author's birthday.

The appearances of Poe's birthday visitor began in the 1940s. His ritual was always the same. Wearing black, he visited the grave after midnight on January 19.

No one ever found out his identity. He would disappear before anyone could ask. He never uttered a sound.

Then, in 2010, the visits stopped. No one knows why. Will the visitor ever reappear? Even Poe could not guess the ending to this mystery!

POSTED BY EMILY MEKLIN AT 8:30 PM

💬 Comment   ✉ Share   ★ Favorite

WORDS TO KNOW!

ritual: an action done the same way each time

Word Count 173   Lexile 580L

🖉 Academic Discussion

Main Idea

Q: What is the main idea of the blog post?

A: The main idea of the blog post is _____.

> An unknown person _____
>
> _____
>
> _____

Important Details

Q: What is known about the mysterious visitor?

A: His _____ was/were _____.

> 1. Visits:
>
> 2. Clothing:
>
> 3. Rituals:

💬 Summarize

Explain the mystery of Poe's birthday visitor. Include the main idea and key details.

Read Primary Sources

Have you ever seen Poe look so **peculiar?** The picture on the left is a caricature. A caricature is a funny drawing of a person. It **exaggerates** certain **features**. Compare the artist Paul Sharp's caricature to a real photo of Poe from 1848. How did Sharp choose to depict him?

Build Word Knowledge

Target Word Read and rate each Target Word.*	Meaning Complete the Target Word meanings.
exaggerate *ex•ag•ger•ate* *(verb)* ☐1 ☐2 ☐3 ☐4	to make something seem _____ or greater than it really is
feature *fea•ture* *(noun)* ☐1 ☐2 ☐3 ☐4	a part of someone's _____

* Rating Scale

1 = I don't know it at all.
2 = I've seen it or heard it.
3 = I think I know the word.
4 = I know it and use it.

🔍 Analyze

Compare the caricature and photo to complete the statements below.

1. What is one feature of Poe's that Sharp chose to exaggerate?

Sharp chose to exaggerate Poe's _____

2. Why did the artist choose to exaggerate this feature?

Sharp exaggerated this feature because _____

_____

3. Poe's most famous writings include a poem called "The Raven" and a short story called "The Black Cat." How is this work reflected in the caricature?

Poe's work is reflected in the caricature _____

_____

_____

TEXT 3
Graphic Novel

📖 Text-Based Questioning

Make Inferences

1. How did the narrator react when he woke up in "a dark, narrow space"?

   The narrator _____

   _____

   _____

2. How did the artist show that the narrator felt this way?

   The artist _____

   _____

   _____

   _____

Vocabulary and Language

3. How does the meaning of the prefix *pre-* help you understand the meaning of *premature* in the title?

   Pre- means _____

   Premature means _____

   _____

   _____

🔍 Word Analysis

Underline the S.M.A.R.T. words with two syllables. Circle the S.M.A.R.T. words with three syllables. Then, divide each S.M.A.R.T. word into syllables.

THE PREMATURE BURIAL

based on the short story by Edgar Allan Poe

The narrator in this short story has one bizarre fear: that he'll accidentally be buried alive. One day he wakes up in a dark, narrow space. Could it be the inside of a coffin?

DARKNESS SURROUNDED ME. WITH HORROR, I REALIZED THAT MY FEARS HAD COME TRUE . . .

I WAS BURIED ALIVE!

WITH A WILD SHRIEK, I CLAWED AT THE WOOD SURROUNDING ME.

WHAT'S WRONG?

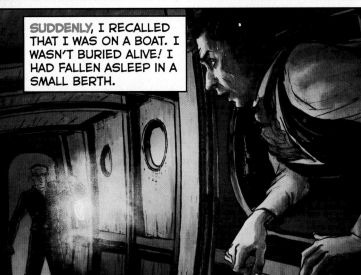

SUDDENLY, I RECALLED THAT I WAS ON A BOAT. I WASN'T BURIED ALIVE! I HAD FALLEN ASLEEP IN A SMALL BERTH.

AFTER THAT NIGHT, I REALIZED THAT FEARING DEATH WAS CAUSING ME TO MISS OUT ON LIFE. FROM THEN ON, I VOWED TO LIVE LIFE FULLY.

Word Count 113   Lexile 440L

Academic Discussion

Main Idea

Q: What is the main idea of the graphic novel?

A: The main idea of the graphic novel is _____.

The narrator loses his fear of premature burial after he _____

_____

Important Details

Q: How did the narrator feel before, during, and after his experience on the boat?

A: _____, the narrator was _____.

1. Before:

2. During:

3. After:

Summarize

Explain why the narrator was so frightened when he woke up. Include the main idea and important details.

Writing Text Type

Literary Analysis

A **literary analysis** examines a text or one element of a text, such as character, plot, setting, or theme in a story.

Read Kavita Webb's analysis of theme in "The Fall of the House of Usher."

Topic Sentence

The **topic sentence** identifies the title, author, and text type that the writer will analyze.

1. **UNDERLINE** the topic sentence.

The topic sentence includes a **controlling idea** about the text or story element being analyzed.

2. **BOX** the **controlling idea**.

Detail Sentences

Detail sentences give supporting **evidence** from the text.

3. ✔ **CHECK** three pieces of supporting **evidence**.

Direct quotations from the text provide evidence for the analysis.

4. **DOUBLE UNDERLINE** a direct quotation.

Language Use

Transition words and phrases introduce and connect ideas.

5. **CIRCLE** two transition words or phrases that introduce or connect ideas.

Concluding Sentence

The **concluding sentence** sums up the writer's ideas about the text.

6. ★ **STAR** the concluding sentence.

Student Model

Friends Are Loyal
by Kavita Webb

One of the themes of the short story "The Fall of the House of Usher," by Edgar Allan Poe, is the importance of friendship. Friends should be loyal and support one another, and that is what the narrator does with his friend Usher. After he receives Usher's letter, the narrator goes to visit his friend, despite the fact that the letter disturbs him. Then, from the moment he arrives, the narrator tries to help Usher. After they glimpse Madeline for what might be the last time, the narrator says he "did everything in my power to lift Usher's spirits" (153). Though the house scares him, the narrator never thinks of abandoning his friend. He even helps Usher bury Madeline. In the end, the narrator cannot save Usher, but by being such a good friend he makes Usher's last days easier.

Brainstorm

Read the writing prompt. Then use the boxes to help you brainstorm ideas.

Characters

Plot

Writing Prompt:
Analyze character, plot, setting, or theme in "The Fall of the House of Usher."

Setting

Theme

Choose Your Topic

Select one of your ideas from the idea web. Then complete the sentences.

I plan to analyze _____ in the short story "The Fall of the

House of Usher" by Edgar Allan Poe. In this story, _____

_____

_____

Organize Ideas for Writing

Complete this outline with notes for your literary analysis.

I. **Topic Sentence.** Identify the title, text type, and author you will analyze.

Topic: _____

Controlling Idea: _____

II. **Detail Sentences.** List evidence that supports the topic sentence.

Detail 1: _____

Detail 2: _____

III. **Concluding Sentence.** Sum up your ideas about the text.

_____

_____

Write Your First Draft

Write your topic sentence.

WORD CHOICES	
Everyday	**Precise**
tells	describes, explains
house	mansion, abode
scary	terrifying, horrific

Topic Sentence

The _____ in the short story "The Fall of the House of Usher"
      (story element)

by Edgar Allan Poe is/are _____
                    (controlling idea)

_____

_____

Type your topic sentence on the computer or write it on paper. Then use these transition words and phrases to help you complete a draft of your literary analysis paragraph.

Detail Sentences

The story takes place in . . .	*The author creates . . .*
In this story, . . .	*Furthermore, . . .*

Concluding Sentence

In summary, . . .	*Overall, . . .*

Revise Your Paragraph

Evaluate: Rate your paragraph. Then have a writing partner rate it.

```
                    Scoring Guide
  needs
improvement   average    good    excellent
     1           2         3          4
```

1. **UNDERLINE** the topic sentence. Does it identify the title, author, and text type being analyzed?

    Self   1   2   3   4
    Partner   1   2   3   4

2. **BOX** the controlling idea. Does it tell what story element the writer will analyze?

    Self   1   2   3   4
    Partner   1   2   3   4

3. ✔**CHECK** the evidence. Does the evidence support the analysis?

    Self   1   2   3   4
    Partner   1   2   3   4

4. **DOUBLE UNDERLINE** the direct quotations. Do they provide evidence for the analysis?

    Self   1   2   3   4
    Partner   1   2   3   4

5. **CIRCLE** transition words and phrases. Do they introduce or connect ideas?

    Self   1   2   3   4
    Partner   1   2   3   4

6. ★**STAR** the concluding sentence. Does it sum up the writer's ideas about the text?

    Self   1   2   3   4
    Partner   1   2   3   4

Discuss: Give feedback on your partner's literary analysis.

1. Start with a positive comment about your partner's literary analysis.

    You did an effective job of _____

    _____

    _____

    _____

2. Give your partner suggestions for revision.

    Your paragraph needs _____

    _____

    _____

    _____

    The evidence would be stronger if ____

    _____

    _____

    _____

3. Answer any questions your partner has about your suggestions.

4. Ask your partner for feedback. Use the frames below to summarize your partner's feedback.

    I did an effective job of . . .
    My paragraph needs . . .
    The evidence would be stronger if I . . .

Revise Now, revise your literary analysis.

Alien INVADERS

How can we stop invader species?

These aliens don't come from outer space. They are pests from other places. These invaders destroy the environment. They must be stopped.

TEXT 1 Magazine Article

KILLING KUDZU

A teen's invention kills an aggressive invader species.

TEXT 2 Patent

Read Primary Sources

Examine a patent for an invention aimed at stopping the spread of kudzu.

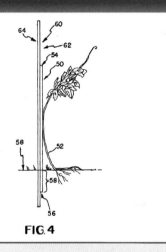

FIG. 4

TEXT 3 News Article

Biosecurity at the Border

Biosecurity specialists keep unwanted species out of the United States.

Using Open and Closed Syllable Strategies

An **open syllable** ends in a vowel and usually has a long vowel sound.

A **closed syllable** ends in a consonant and usually has a short vowel sound.

Open or Closed?

Underline the vowel spots in each word. Circle the words that begin with open syllables. Underline the words that begin with closed syllables.

1. h͟o͟t͟e͟l

2. plastic

3. button

4. human

5. recent

6. public

7. napkin

8. jacket

9. basic

10. cricket

11. raven

12. travel

Analyze Words

Draw a line to divide each word into syllables. Write the syllables on the lines. (Circle) each open syllable.

1. dis|gust   _dis_   _gust_

2. silent   _____   _____

3. recent   _____   _____

4. constant   _____   _____

5. talent   _____   _____

6. focus   _____   _____

7. happen   _____   _____

8. label   _____   _____

Sentence Solver

Blend the syllables to read the words. Write the correct word in each blank.

plas tic	fu ture	traf fic
mu sic	blan ket	se cret

1. My new computer has a red _____ cover.

2. We were late because of _____

3. In the _____ I want to visit my grandparents.

4. I wear headphones when I listen to _____

5. Can you keep a _____

6. Bring a _____ in case it gets cold.

📖 Text-Based Questioning

Cause and Effect

1. Why is Jacob Schindler's invention so important?

   Jacob Schindler's invention is important

   because _____

   _____

   _____

   _____

2. How does Schindler's invention work?

   Schindler's invention _____

   _____

   _____

   _____

   _____

Vocabulary & Language

3. Why does the writer describe kudzu as a "monster" in paragraph 1?

   Kudzu is described as a "monster"

   because _____

   _____

   _____

🔍 Word Analysis

Circle the S.M.A.R.T. words that have a closed first syllable. Underline the words that have an open first syllable.

INVENTOR OF THE MONTH

KUDZU CONQUEROR
Jacob shows off the steel bit he uses to pump helium into the ground.

KILLING KUDZU

by Jordan Gary

A teenager's invention kills an aggressive invader species.

A green monster has **invaded** the South. It covers thousands of miles. It grows up to a foot a day. People slash and burn it. But it always grows back.

This monster is the kudzu vine. It is native to China and Japan. People in the United States began planting kudzu in 1876. Farmers liked kudzu at first because it kept soil from washing away and provided food for livestock. But soon it grew out of control.

Jacob Schindler, 17, discovered how to kill kudzu. He lives in Georgia, where kudzu is a huge problem.

While brainstorming ideas for a science project, Jacob wondered if he could kill kudzu without hurting any other plants or animals. He wanted to know if gas would kill kudzu.

Jacob pumped different gases through a tube and into the ground near the kudzu roots. He tried nitrous oxide, oxygen, carbon dioxide, and helium. Helium worked. It was **poisonous** to kudzu, but did not interfere with the rest of the **environment**. The kudzu quickly died and did not grow back. Then, Jacob designed a hollow steel bit that drills into the ground. This invention makes it easier to pump helium near the kudzu roots.

Jacob fights kudzu, but he also looks for ways the vine could benefit humans. He experiments with different recipes that use kudzu. Would you eat a kudzu salad?

WORDS TO KNOW!

hollow: empty inside

bit: a metal tool that is inserted into a drill and used to make a hole

Word Count 227   Lexile 740L

⑨ Academic Discussion

Main Idea

Q: What is the main idea of the article?

A: The main idea of the article is _____.

| Jacob Schindler invented a way _____ _____ |

Important Details

Q: How does Jacob fight kudzu?

A: To fight kudzu, Jacob uses _____ to _____.

1. A steel bit:

2. Helium:

⑨ Summarize

Explain how Jacob's invention kills kudzu. Include the main idea and important details.

Read Primary Sources

A lock protects belongings, but how are ideas protected? With a patent! Inventors like Jacob Schindler apply for patents to keep other people from stealing their ideas. Patents give inventors the **exclusive** right to make or sell their inventions. Below is a patent for another kudzu-fighting **method**. **Barriers** are placed near areas where kudzu grows. The kudzu vine cannot attach to the barriers. Because of this, the vines cannot grow any further in that direction.

(12) **United States Patent**	(10) **Patent No.:**	**US 6,684,578 B1**
Callahan	(45) **Date of Patent:**	**Feb. 3, 2004**

(54) **KUDZU CONTROL METHOD AND APPARATUS**

(76) Inventor: **Jack Newell Callahan**

(*) Notice: Subject to any disclaimer, the term of this patent is extended or adjusted under 35 U.S.C. 154(b) by 0 days.

(21) Appl. No.: **10/316,634**

(22) Filed: **Dec. 10, 2002**

Related U.S. Application Data

(60) Provisional application No. 60/369,679, filed on Apr. 2, 2002, and provisional application No. 60/353,751, filed on Jan. 31, 2002.

(51) Int. Cl.[7] **H02G 7/00**; A01G 13/00
(52) U.S. Cl. **52/147**; 47/32.5
(58) Field of Search .... 47/20.1, 23.1, 47/23.2, 32.4, 32.5, 58.1 R; 52/147, 101

(56) **References Cited**

U.S. PATENT DOCUMENTS

428,206 A	*	5/1890	Fouquet	47/32.4
494,874 A	*	4/1893	Majola	47/32.4
1,938,957 A	*	12/1933	Fox	74/127
1,994,101 A	*	3/1935	Hawkins	43/108
2,003,959 A	*	6/1935	St. John	52/147
2,061,306 A	*	11/1936	Hocher et al.	52/147
2,264,430 A	*	12/1941	Bierce	52/147
3,333,361 A	*	8/1967	Manak	47/58.1
3,531,900 A	*	10/1970	Vaughn	52/10
4,244,156 A	*	1/1981	Watts, Jr.	52/746.1
6,223,463 B1	*	5/2001	Carlson et al.	43/108
6,226,933 B1	*	5/2001	Nelson et al.	52/101

FOREIGN PATENT DOCUMENTS

| JP | 11-355946 | * 12/1999 | H02G/7/00 |

OTHER PUBLICATIONS

Clayton, Ron. Aug. 31, 2002. New device may control kudzu. Chattanooga Times Free Press: p. A1.*
Kudzu Management Program: Containing the Spread and ... and Potential Solution.

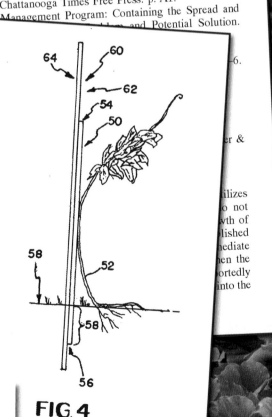

FIG. 4

Figure 4 (right) shows a kudzu vine falling away from the barrier.

Build Word Knowledge

Target Word Read and rate each Target Word.*	Meaning Complete the Target Word meanings.
exclusive ex•clu•sive *(adjective)* 1 2 3 4	available or _____ to a particular person or group
barrier bar•ri•er *(noun)* 1 2 3 4	a physical object that sets an area _____

* Rating Scale	1 = I don't know it at all.	3 = I think I know the word.
	2 = I've seen it or heard it.	4 = I know it and use it.

Analyze

Use the patent to answer the questions below.

1. What is the name of this invention?

The invention is called _____

_____

2. Who is the inventor?

The inventor is _____

3. How is this invention different from Jacob Schindler's?

This invention _____

_____

_____

_____

_____

Text-Based Questioning

Cause and Effect

1. What causes specialists to quarantine a shipment?

   They quarantine a shipment if _____

   _____

   _____

   _____

2. What can happen if a disease or pest enters the United States?

   Pests can _____

   _____

   _____

   _____

Vocabulary & Language

3. If someone who works in biosecurity protects living things, what does the prefix *bio-* mean?

   The prefix *bio-* _____

   _____

   _____

Word Analysis

Circle the S.M.A.R.T. words that have a closed first syllable. Underline the words that have an open first syllable.

TOWN TRIBUNE **NATIONAL**

Biosecurity at the Border

By JACKIE CONNER

The day starts early at the Miami Plant Inspection Station in Miami, Florida. There, biosecurity specialists are ready to inspect a shipment of citrus plants that has arrived from Indonesia.

These **capable** specialists work for the U.S. Department of Agriculture. They are **responsible** for protecting the United States. Shipments from other countries can contain diseases and pests. These can invade and **threaten** American crops.

The specialists' day is busy. But they know they have an important job.

First, the specialists check the permits for the shipment. These papers show that the shipment has permission to enter the United States. They examine the shipment. They look for signs of invader species.

One specialist sees something. Some of the plants look yellow and blotchy. They may have a disease called citrus greening. The bug that spreads this disease is only about 3 mm long. But the devastation it causes is huge.

Agents inspect a shipment for dangerous species.

Trees infected with citrus greening produce fruit that is deformed and bitter. There is no cure. The trees die in just a few years. About 65% of citrus fruits in the United States come from Florida, so the specialists at the Miami station are on alert for any trouble.

The crew decides that the whole shipment will be quarantined for testing. If citrus greening is found, the shipment will be destroyed.

The specialists' day is busy. But they know they have an important job: protecting the United States from dangerous invaders.

WORDS TO KNOW!

shipment: a load of goods sent by sea, road, or air

quarantined: isolated or put aside because of a disease or infection

Word Count **227** Lexile **660L**

Academic Discussion

Main Idea

Q: What is the main idea of the article?

A: The main idea of the article is _____.

> Biosecurity specialists _____
>
> _____
>
> _____

Important Details

Q: How do biosecurity specialists handle the shipment of citrus plants?

A: The inspectors _____ to _____.

1. Check permits:

2. Examine the shipment:

3. Quarantine the shipment:

Summarize

Explain how biosecurity specialists protect the United States. Include the main idea and important details.

Writing Text Type

Argument Paragraph

An **argument** states a position or claim about an issue. The writer supports the claim with convincing evidence and reasons.

Read Shanta Gupta's argument paragraph about a harmful invader species.

Topic Sentence

The **topic sentence** introduces an issue.

1. **UNDERLINE** the topic sentence.

The topic sentence also presents the writer's **claim**, or position, about the issue.

2. **BOX** the claim.

Detail Sentences

Convincing reasons and relevant evidence support the claim.

3. ✔ **CHECK** two reasons or pieces of evidence.

A strong argument points out weaknesses in **opposing arguments**.

4. → **PUT AN ARROW** next to an opposing argument.

Language Use

Transition words and phrases introduce and connect ideas.

5. **CIRCLE** four transition words or phrases.

Concluding Sentence

The **conclusion** restates the claim and offers a recommendation.

6. ★ **STAR** the concluding sentence.

Student Model

Stop the Zebra Mussel!
by Shanta Gupta

I believe that zebra mussels are the most harmful invader species. One reason is that zebra mussels hurt the food chain in the Great Lakes area. They eat the food that other fish need to survive, and the other fish die as a result. In addition, zebra mussels harm people's ability to earn a living. If many fish die, then fishers will catch and sell fewer fish. Some people may argue that zebra mussels affect a small area and are not a dangerous threat. However, any threat to the food chain is very serious. In conclusion, zebra mussels negatively affect both animals and people, which is why I urge everyone to write to his or her elected officials and ask that more money be spent to stop this invader species.

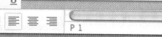

Brainstorm

Read the writing prompt. Then use the boxes to help you brainstorm ideas.

Invader 1	Invader 2

Writing Prompt:
Write an argument paragraph about the most harmful plant or animal invader. Support your argument with evidence from the Workshop readings.

Invader 3	Invader 4

State Your Position

Use ideas from your idea web to help you determine your position. Then complete the sentences.

I will argue that _____

because _____

_____

Organize Ideas for Writing

Complete this outline with notes for your argument paragraph.

I. Topic Sentence Introduce the issue and your claim about it.

Issue: _____

Claim: _____

II. Detail Sentences List evidence or reasons that support your claim.

Detail 1: _____

Detail 2: _____

III. Concluding Sentence Restate your claim and make a recommendation.

In summary, _____

_____

Write Your First Draft

Write your topic sentence.

WORD CHOICES	
Everyday	**Precise**
freaky	strange, unusual
poison	venom
grow	sprout, expand

Topic Sentence

I believe that the most harmful invader species is _____ (topic)

because _____ (claim)

_____

_____

Type your topic sentence on the computer or write it on paper. Then use some of these transition words and phrases to complete a draft of your paragraph.

Detail Sentences

One reason is . . .	Another reason . . .
In addition . . .	Finally . . .

Concluding Sentence

For these reasons . . .	In conclusion . . .

Revise Your Paragraph

Evaluate: Rate your argument paragraph. Then have a writing partner rate it.

Scoring Guide			
needs improvement	average	good	excellent
1	2	3	4

1. **<u>UNDERLINE</u>** the topic sentence. Does it introduce the issue clearly?

   Self   1   2   3   4

   Partner   1   2   3   4

2. **BOX** the claim. Does it express the writer's claim?

   Self   1   2   3   4

   Partner   1   2   3   4

3. **✔CHECK** the reasons and evidence. Are they convincing and relevant?

   Self   1   2   3   4

   Partner   1   2   3   4

4. **→ PUT AN ARROW** next to an opposing argument. Does the paragraph point out a weakness?

   Self   1   2   3   4

   Partner   1   2   3   4

5. **CIRCLE** transition words and phrases. Do they connect ideas?

   Self   1   2   3   4

   Partner   1   2   3   4

6. **★STAR** the conclusion. Does it offer a recommendation?

   Self   1   2   3   4

   Partner   1   2   3   4

Discuss: Give feedback on your partner's argument paragraph.

1. Start with a positive comment about your partner's argument paragraph.

   I found your argument convincing

   because _____

   _____

   _____

2. Give your partner suggestions for revision.

   Your argument would be stronger if ___

   _____

   _____

   Your paragraph needs _____

   _____

   _____

3. Answer any questions your partner has about your suggestions.

4. Ask your partner for feedback. Use the frames below to summarize your partner's feedback.

   You found my argument convincing because . . .

   My argument would be stronger if . . .

   My paragraph needs . . .

Revise: Now, revise your argument paragraph.

Turning Points

What does it mean to be "at a turning point"?

A turning point means getting ready for something totally new and different. How do people face these turning points?

TEXT 1 Newsletter

LEGAL GRAFFITI

Young people create murals instead of graffiti.

TEXT 2 Mural

Read Primary Sources

Analyze the work done by students in a community mural program.

TEXT 3 Magazine Article

The Accidental
Artist

A medical emergency changed the way Jon Sarkin sees the world.

Using Approximation

Put your tablet on the table.

Sometimes, you need to try different strategies and pronunciations to read new words.

Sound out a word with the stress on different syllables, or break the syllables in different places until the word sounds right.

Mark It

Draw a line between the syllables. (Circle) the stressed syllable. Pronounce the word, using approximation.

1. magic

3. flavor

5. puzzle

2. before

4. subtract

6. surprise

Split It

Break the words into syllables. Use approximation to read the words. (Circle) the syllables with schwa sounds.

1. random _____ _____

4. circus _____ _____

2. agree _____ _____

5. avoid _____ _____

3. happen _____ _____

6. excellent _____ _____ _____

Sort It

Write each word from the word list in the correct box. The first one is done for you.

drastic	lilac	label	final	cotton	solo
dental	photo	infant	connect	control	allow

Short Vowel First Syllable	Long Vowel First Syllable	Schwa First Syllable
drastic		

Word Hunt

Fill in the missing word in each sentence. Find the word in the list.

1. The parents brought their new _____ home from the hospital.

2. Our team played in the _____ game, but we lost the tournament.

3. Don't forget to _____ your computer to a power source.

4. I took a great _____ of my cat with my new cell phone.

5. You have to learn to _____ your speed on a skateboard.

6. I had a _____ emergency when I knocked out my two front teeth.

Text-Based Questioning

Compare and Contrast

1. How was Sarkin different after his stroke?

_____

_____

_____

_____

_____

2. How did art help Sarkin after his stroke?

_____

_____

_____

_____

Vocabulary & Language

3. Why does the author write that Sarkin is "compelled" to draw in paragraph 5?

_____

_____

_____

_____

Word Analysis

Circle the S.M.A.R.T. words that start with a stressed syllable. Underline the words that start with an unstressed syllable.

The Accidental Artist

Art helps one man cope with a *new life.*

by Jeff Ortiz

Jon Sarkin knows what it is like to wake up feeling like a different person. More than 20 years ago, he suffered a stroke when a blood vessel in his brain burst. To fix it, his doctor had to remove a piece of his cerebellum, a part of the brain that controls the muscles. This saved Sarkin's life, but it also changed it **dramatically**.

The changes the stroke had caused became clear as Sarkin recovered. He was deaf in one ear and had double vision. Balancing was difficult, so he needed a cane to walk. His personality had changed as well. He was no longer interested in his work as a chiropractor. Once personable, he was now withdrawn.

Strangest of all, Sarkin had an overwhelming urge to draw. He filled page after page with swirls of color, sketches of objects, and storms of scribbles and shapes. He could not stop.

Because of the changes to his brain, Sarkin saw the world differently. He could no longer understand things as a whole. Thoughts came to him in flashes and pieces. Art helped him create order and make sense of the world.

Today, Sarkin still feels compelled to create art. He works as a professional artist. His drawings and paintings are shown in galleries across the world. People pay as much as $10,000 to buy one of his pieces. But the money is not why Sarkin works as an artist. Creating art is not just his job; it is his life.

WORDS TO KNOW!

double vision: a medical condition where a person sees two of every object at all times

urge: a strong need

Word Count **249**   Lexile **690L**

Academic Discussion

Main Idea
Q: What is the main idea of the article?
A: The main idea of the article is _____.

_____
_____
_____

Important Details
Q: How did the stroke change Sarkin's life?
A: _____ the stroke, Sarkin _____.

1. Before:

2. After:

Summarize

Explain why Jon Sarkin became an accidental artist.

THE STREETS OF HARLEM

What was Harlem like in the past? What is it like now?

In the 1920s, Harlem became the
heartbeat of African-American culture.
Its rich heritage is still valued today.

TEXT 1 Web Page

THE TREE OF HOPE

Generations of performers have turned to a special tree for good luck.

TEXT 2 Poem

Read Primary Sources

Analyze the revisions Langston Hughes made to one of his famous poems.

BALLAD OF BOOKER T.
by
Langston Hughes

~~Old~~ Booker T.
Was a practical man.
He said, Till the soi
And learn from the la
Let down your bucket
Where you are;

TEXT 3 News Article

The Changing Face of Harlem's "Main Street"

Are chain stores threatening the legacy of 125th Street?

Recognizing Word Families

I'm going down to the basement to look for some base words.

I think you already found the **base** word in **basement**!

A **base word** is a word to which other word parts, like prefixes, suffixes, and endings, may be added.

A **base word family** is the group of words that share the same base word.

Sometimes you can figure out the meaning of a word if you think about another word from the same family.

Mark It

Underline the base words. **Circle** the prefixes, suffixes, and endings.

1. helpful

3. slowly

5. preschool

2. reread

4. unwanted

6. uncommonness

Write It

Underline the base word. **Circle** the prefix or suffix. Write the word's meaning.

1. preview _____

2. replay _____

3. saddest _____

4. skillful _____

5. misbehave _____

6. unkind _____

Sort It

Underline the base words in the word list. Then, write the base words at the top of the chart. Sort the words by base word family.

unkind	unevenness	kindly	kindness
friendly	unfriendly	uneven	evenly
unkindly	unfriendliness	friendliness	evenness

kind	_____	_____

Sentence Solver

Choose the correct word from the word list to fill in each blank.

1. It was difficult to ride our bikes because of the _____ of the road.

2. The dog's owner said it was safe to pet it because it was a _____ animal.

3. The basketball game was exciting because the teams were

_____ matched.

4. Helping an older person carry heavy bags is an act of _____

5. Tom was elected president of the class because of his _____ to everyone.

SYSTEM
44
*NEXT*GENERATION

Success Passages

Series 1 — Bats Do That?

Baby bats are everywhere! Bat moms can find them. They use sound signals. They use smell signals. Their communication is amazing! The baby bats eat. The baby bats get big!

9
18
27
30

Series 2 — Art for Kicks

Steven is an artist. He picks a shoe. He dips his brush. He dabs on a design!

12
17

Kids pick shoes. They pick their favorite kicks. They pick kicks that fit.

26
30

Are you creative? Can you paint kicks?

37

Series 3 — Run, Jesse, Run

Jesse Owens ran track for the USA. In 1936, he went to Germany to run in the Olympics. The German dictator Hitler said Jesse could not win. But Jesse was quick. His team could count on him.

11
20
30
37

Jesse wanted to win. And he did. He got four gold medals. He demonstrated that he was the fastest man alive.

48
56
58

Series 4 — Passing the Sniff Test

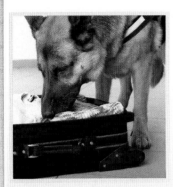

Some dogs have a special skill. They can smell trouble! 10
They do sniff tests. They can detect bombs and guns. 20
Dogs take big risks to help people. Good job, dogs! 30

Series 5 — Brain Freeze

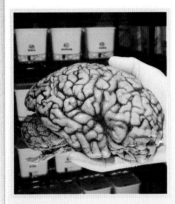

What is a brain bank? People drop off brains. 9
Scientists use them for research. 14

Luis is a brain scientist. He grabs a brain. He splits it 26
into bits. He looks at the bits under glass in his lab. 38

Want a plan for your brain? You can deposit it at a 50
brain bank! 52

Series 6 — King of the Court

Pancho Gonzales grew up in the 1940s and 1950s. 9
Back then, most tennis camps and clubs were just for 19
whites. Mexican Americans like Pancho had little 26
chance to take lessons. 30

So Pancho decided to teach himself. He practiced 38
hard. He was determined to be the best. 46

Pancho became a fantastic player. He had a very rapid 56
serve. He got to the top rank in tennis. Pancho was king 68
of the court! 71

| Series 7 | ## Something Fishy |

Vets rush to help a sick pet. They do surgery. They stitch up its chest. What's the catch? This patient is just a fish. 11 / 22 / 24

Some people might just flush a sick fish. Others spend lots of cash on medical help. They love pet fish! 34 / 44

| Series 8 | ## High-Flying Circus |

Check out this school. You might be shocked. This is not a typical school. It's a circus school. 10 / 18

Kids do math and spelling. But the big subjects are flipping and twisting. Kids practice jumping and catching. They do thrilling tricks, too. 27 / 35 / 41

These kids are on the path to jobs in the circus! 52

| Series 9 | ## Struggle for Survival |

A leopard has a problem. He lets his lunch tumble from a branch. A hyena snatches it in her powerful jaws. The leopard wants it back. The animals struggle. 10 / 21 / 29

A lioness brings the struggle to an end. Her size is her advantage. The other animals run from her. The lioness grabs the lunch in an instant. 41 / 50 / 56

Series 10 — Live From the Hive

Sometimes, hornets attack! They dive inside a hive. They kill the bees. They take the honey. 8 / 16

How do hornets do this? First, a single hornet races to the hive. It tags the hive with a special smell. Then other hornets can sniff out the hive. 27 / 39 / 45

But this plan only works when the first hornet escapes with its life. Sometimes, bees stage the first strike. They signal each other. They surround the hornet. Then they vibrate together. 55 / 65 / 74 / 76

The bees bake the hornet alive. What a punishment! 85

Series 11 — Hero of Hope

Emmanuel lives in Ghana. He is missing a bone in his right leg. In Ghana, people like him often got rejected. Some felt that they were unable to contribute. 11 / 21 / 29

Emmanuel decided to demonstrate what he could do. He taught himself to ride a bike. He used just his left leg to ride. He rode 379 miles across Ghana. 37 / 50 / 58

Huge crowds came to see Emmanuel ride. His amazing ride changed minds about the disabled. Emmanuel gave hope to disabled people. 66 / 73 / 79

| Series 12 | **Up and Running** |

Ordinary life can be challenging for kids who live | 9
in difficult places. Some teachers in California offered | 17
a bunch of kids a new kind of challenge. They invited | 28
them to run a marathon. That's a 26-mile race! | 37

Getting fit for the race was difficult. Some kids | 46
disliked it at first. They thought about quitting. But in | 56
time, they were running many miles. | 62

The day of the big race came. Fifty-four kids jogged | 72
across the finish line! That's just the beginning. | 80
What else will they do with hard work and the desire | 91
for success? | 93

| Series 13 | **Flies That Spy** |

Spy planes are huge. They fly high so no one will | 11
notice them. They take snapshots of cities below. | 19

But what if you hoped to spy inside buildings? You | 29
would need tiny planes. Luckily, engineers are trying to | 38
develop them. | 40

The new generation of planes may look like insects. | 49
Their wings will flap like flies' wings. They will whiz | 59
into buildings. They will buzz around computers and | 67
phones. They will go places big spy planes can't! | 76

Robots: Now It's Personal

Cynthia makes complex robots. She makes robots that 8
behave like humans. Real human babies are the basis of 18
her designs. She uses her baby as a model. 27

Cynthia made a robot named Leo. When she chats 36
with him, Leo focuses on her face. He can recognize 46
her emotions. 48

Take a moment to chat with Leo. You might forget 58
that he is a machine! 63

Hail to the Chef

Step inside the White House kitchen. The head chef 9
is the person who maintains it. And Cris was the first 20
woman hired to do that job. 26

What's expected of the top chef? Every day, she makes 36
perfect meals for powerful people. She uses her training 45
in cooking. She manages the kitchen, too. She must stay 55
on top of every detail. 60

Does that sound stressful? It is! But every detail 69
is important when the President is waiting for a 78
daily snack! 80

Series 16	**Going Coastal**

The city of Dubai roasts in the desert sun. But its ruler   12
had a goal. He would create a new coastal area. People   23
could go there to cool off.   29

Workers sucked up sand from below the sea. They   38
used it to form islands shaped like palm trees.   47

The Palm Islands development was made to impress   55
people. It boasts hundreds of homes, hotels, and shops.   64
It has sandy beaches for swimming and boating.   72

The price tag may impress you, too. Dubai spent tens   82
of billions to create these islands!   88

Series 17	**The Dream Team**

Aniak, Alaska, is a village deep in the Alaskan wild.   10
What happens when there is a major emergency? A   19
team of teens rushes to help. Aniak has no cash to pay   31
an adult rescue crew. So local teens agreed to be trained   42
as volunteers.   44

In the wild, victims can be difficult to reach. The   54
teens sometimes travel by truck or speedboat. They   62
might even need a plane. But this dream team can't be   73
defeated. They will do anything they can to save lives.   83

Series 18 — Get Ready to Roll!

New Zealand is a land of extreme sports. The latest fad 11
is a giant plastic bubble. The objective is to step inside 22
and roll. It's a wild ride! 28

Riders can use their feet to set their own pace. Or, 39
they can fold themselves inside the bubble high on a hill. 50
They get a push. Then they hang on tightly as they roll to 63
the bottom at a frightening rate! 69

The rolling sensation is catching on everywhere. Are 77
you ready to roll? 81

Series 19 — Shark Attack?

Something was killing the dogfish sharks in the tank 9
at the big fish exhibit. Sharks are large and have sharp 20
teeth. They are expert killers. So, what was killing them? 30
No one was certain. 34

The only other large animal in the tank was an 44
octopus. And an octopus usually eats small animals, like 53
crabs and shrimp. It was a murder mystery. 61

A camera was set up to observe the tank. It revealed 72
the octopus killing a shark. The shark murder mystery 81
was solved. 83

Back in Action

Technology can help make life more enjoyable for 8
amputees. For example, new materials make artificial 15
limbs flexible and light. People who use these limbs 24
can take a stroll without discomfort. Feet shaped for 33
running give athletes cause for celebration. Computer 40
chips make artificial joints highly adjustable. 46

Juan has the world's first bionic hand. First, he moves 56
his biceps. Electrodes in the hand detect the movement. 65
They send a message to the fingers. The information tells 75
the fingers what to do. 80

Technology keeps moving forward. That means 86
disabled people can keep moving forward, too. 93

Dear Reader: 2

You have mastered the system! Can I get your   11
autograph?   12

On your way through the four parts of the system,   22
you have seen videos starring baby bats, tennis champs,   31
social robots, dancing clowns, and more. Today, you are   40
the star.   42

What did it take to transport yourself across the finish   52
line of this program? You needed hard work, intelligence,   61
and the perseverance to keep going—even when you felt   71
like you might never crack the code.   78

Where will you go from here? Only you can decide.   88
But I predict great things for your future!   96

Best wishes,   98

Ivan   99

My Achievements

My Individual Learning Plan: Behavioral Goals Rubric

Responsibility

👥 Whole Group	👥 Small Group	
Arrive on time.	Transition to small group quickly and quietly.	
Bring your *44Book*, Do Now Log, and a pencil or pen.	Bring your *44Book* and a pencil or pen.	
Complete the Do Now immediately.	Begin assigned tasks immediately.	
Be prepared to answer teacher's questions.	Be prepared to answer teacher's questions.	
Points ① ② ③ ④	① ② ③ ④	

Respect

👥 Whole Group	👥 Small Group	
Listen actively with your eyes and ears.	Listen actively with your eyes and ears.	
Use kind words, polite tone, and appropriate language.	Use kind words, polite tone, and appropriate language.	
Share materials when appropriate.	Share materials when appropriate.	
Leave whole-group area clean and organized.	Leave small-group area clean and organized.	
Points ① ② ③ ④	① ② ③ ④	

Effort

👥 Whole Group	👥 Small Group	
Complete Do Now and Wrap Up with accuracy and care.	Complete *44Book* and RDI tasks with accuracy and care.	
Pay attention to directions and details.	Pay attention to directions and details.	
Ignore distractions.	Ignore distractions.	
Keep trying!	Complete My *44Book* Response Log and keep trying!	
Points ① ② ③ ④	① ② ③ ④	

Week of _____

📖 Independent Reading	💻 Software	
Transition to independent reading quickly and quietly.	Transition to your computer quickly and quietly.	
Choose a paperback, eBook, or Audiobook.	Find your designated work station.	
Begin reading immediately.	Log into your computer immediately.	
Be prepared to think and write.	Be prepared to answer the questions on the software.	**Total Points:** /16
① ② ③ ④	① ② ③ ④	

📖 Independent Reading	💻 Software	
Stay focused on your own book.	Work on the computer independently and allow others to work independently.	
Find new books without distracting others.	Use appropriate voice level when reading aloud.	
Treat books with care and use them respectfully.	Use materials (keyboard, monitor, headphones, mouse) carefully.	
Return book to designated area when you are done with it.	Leave the computer work station clean and organized.	**Total Points:** /16
① ② ③ ④	① ② ③ ④	

📖 Independent Reading	💻 Software	
Pay careful attention to your reading.	Work on the software for 15 minutes a day.	
Look up words you don't understand.	Speak clearly and naturally when reading aloud.	
Ignore distractions.	Ignore distractions.	
Complete Reading Logs and QuickWrite.	Use the dashboard and My Software Tracking Log to monitor your software and reading progress.	**Total Points:** /16
① ② ③ ④	① ② ③ ④	

Total Points: /48

My Individual Learning Plan: Behavioral Goals Rubric

Responsibility

👥 Whole Group	👥 Small Group	
Arrive on time.	Transition to small group quickly and quietly.	
Bring your *44Book*, Do Now Log, and a pencil or pen.	Bring your *44Book* and a pencil or pen.	
Complete the Do Now immediately.	Begin assigned tasks immediately.	
Be prepared to answer teacher's questions.	Be prepared to answer teacher's questions.	
Points ① ② ③ ④	① ② ③ ④	

Respect

👥 Whole Group	👥 Small Group	
Listen actively with your eyes and ears.	Listen actively with your eyes and ears.	
Use kind words, polite tone, and appropriate language.	Use kind words, polite tone, and appropriate language.	
Share materials when appropriate.	Share materials when appropriate.	
Leave whole-group area clean and organized.	Leave small-group area clean and organized.	
Points ① ② ③ ④	① ② ③ ④	

Effort

👥 Whole Group	👥 Small Group	
Complete Do Now and Wrap Up with accuracy and care.	Complete *44Book* and RDI tasks with accuracy and care.	
Pay attention to directions and details.	Pay attention to directions and details.	
Ignore distractions.	Ignore distractions.	
Keep trying!	Complete My *44Book* Response Log and keep trying!	
Points ① ② ③ ④	① ② ③ ④	

Week of _____

📖 Independent Reading	💻 Software	
Transition to independent reading quickly and quietly.	Transition to your computer quickly and quietly.	
Choose a paperback, eBook, or Audiobook.	Find your designated work station.	
Begin reading immediately.	Log into your computer immediately.	
Be prepared to think and write.	Be prepared to answer the questions on the software.	**Total Points:** /16
① ② ③ ④	① ② ③ ④	

📖 Independent Reading	💻 Software	
Stay focused on your own book.	Work on the computer independently and allow others to work independently.	
Find new books without distracting others.	Use appropriate voice level when reading aloud.	
Treat books with care and use them respectfully.	Use materials (keyboard, monitor, headphones, mouse) carefully.	
Return book to designated area when you are done with it.	Leave the computer work station clean and organized.	**Total Points:** /16
① ② ③ ④	① ② ③ ④	

📖 Independent Reading	💻 Software	
Pay careful attention to your reading.	Work on the software for 15 minutes a day.	
Look up words you don't understand.	Speak clearly and naturally when reading aloud.	
Ignore distractions.	Ignore distractions.	
Complete Reading Logs and QuickWrite.	Use the dashboard and My Software Tracking Log to monitor your software and reading progress.	**Total Points:** /16
① ② ③ ④	① ② ③ ④	

Total Points:	**/48**

My Individual Learning Plan: Behavioral Goals Rubric

👥 Whole Group	👥 Small Group	
Responsibility		
Arrive on time.	Transition to small group quickly and quietly.	
Bring your *44Book*, Do Now Log, and a pencil or pen.	Bring your *44Book* and a pencil or pen.	
Complete the Do Now immediately.	Begin assigned tasks immediately.	
Be prepared to answer teacher's questions.	Be prepared to answer teacher's questions.	
Points ① ② ③ ④	① ② ③ ④	

👥 Whole Group	👥 Small Group	
Respect		
Listen actively with your eyes and ears.	Listen actively with your eyes and ears.	
Use kind words, polite tone, and appropriate language.	Use kind words, polite tone, and appropriate language.	
Share materials when appropriate.	Share materials when appropriate.	
Leave whole-group area clean and organized.	Leave small-group area clean and organized.	
Points ① ② ③ ④	① ② ③ ④	

👥 Whole Group	👥 Small Group	
Effort		
Complete Do Now and Wrap Up with accuracy and care.	Complete *44Book* and RDI tasks with accuracy and care.	
Pay attention to directions and details.	Pay attention to directions and details.	
Ignore distractions.	Ignore distractions.	
Keep trying!	Complete My *44Book* Response Log and keep trying!	
Points ① ② ③ ④	① ② ③ ④	

Week of _____

📖 Independent Reading	💻 Software	
Transition to independent reading quickly and quietly.	Transition to your computer quickly and quietly.	
Choose a paperback, eBook, or Audiobook.	Find your designated work station.	
Begin reading immediately.	Log into your computer immediately.	
Be prepared to think and write.	Be prepared to answer the questions on the software.	**Total Points:** /16
① ② ③ ④	① ② ③ ④	

📖 Independent Reading	💻 Software	
Stay focused on your own book.	Work on the computer independently and allow others to work independently.	
Find new books without distracting others.	Use appropriate voice level when reading aloud.	
Treat books with care and use them respectfully.	Use materials (keyboard, monitor, headphones, mouse) carefully.	
Return book to designated area when you are done with it.	Leave the computer work station clean and organized.	**Total Points:** /16
① ② ③ ④	① ② ③ ④	

📖 Independent Reading	💻 Software	
Pay careful attention to your reading.	Work on the software for 15 minutes a day.	
Look up words you don't understand.	Speak clearly and naturally when reading aloud.	
Ignore distractions.	Ignore distractions.	
Complete Reading Logs and QuickWrite.	Use the dashboard and My Software Tracking Log to monitor your software and reading progress.	**Total Points:** /16
① ② ③ ④	① ② ③ ④	

Total Points: /48

My Conferences

Complete the information each time you conference with your teacher.
★Star one item you are proud of. (Circle) one item you want to improve.

CONFERENCE 1

Date: _____ Current Topic: _____

Words Read: _____ Median Session Time: _____

Decoding Fluency Score: _____ *Reading Counts!* Average Quiz Score: _____

Small-Group Participation: _____

Discuss Academic Goals

	My Goal	**Actual**
Decoding	_____ Topics Completed	_____ Topics Completed
Spelling	_____ Spelling Challenge	_____ Spelling Challenge
Comprehension	_____ Books Read	_____ Books Read

Celebrate Success

I am proud of _____

I have done well in this part of *System 44* because _____

_____

Reflect

I am struggling with _____

This is challenging because _____

Teacher Comments: _____

_____

CONFERENCE 2

Date: _____ Current Topic: _____

Words Read: _____ Median Session Time: _____

Decoding Fluency Score: _____ *Reading Counts!* Average Quiz Score: _____

Small-Group Participation: _____

Discuss Academic Goals

	My Goal	**Actual**
Decoding	_____ Topics Completed	_____ Topics Completed
Spelling	_____ Spelling Challenge	_____ Spelling Challenge
Comprehension	_____ Books Read	_____ Books Read

Celebrate Success

I am proud of _____

I have done well in this part of *System 44* because _____

_____

Reflect

I am struggling with _____

This is challenging because _____

Teacher Comments: _____

_____

☆ GOALS

CONFERENCE 3

Date: _____ Current Topic: _____

Words Read: _____ Median Session Time: _____

Decoding Fluency Score: _____ *Reading Counts!* Average Quiz Score: _____

Small-Group Participation: _____

Discuss Academic Goals

	My Goal	**Actual**
Decoding	_____ Topics Completed	_____ Topics Completed
Spelling	_____ Spelling Challenge	_____ Spelling Challenge
Comprehension	_____ Books Read	_____ Books Read

Celebrate Success

I am proud of _____

I have done well in this part of *System 44* because _____

_____

Reflect

I am struggling with _____

This is challenging because _____

Teacher Comments: _____

_____

CONFERENCE 4

Date: _____ Current Topic: _____

Words Read: _____ Median Session Time: _____

Decoding Fluency Score: _____ *Reading Counts!* Average Quiz Score: _____

Small-Group Participation: _____

Discuss Academic Goals

	My Goal	**Actual**
Decoding	_____ Topics Completed	_____ Topics Completed
Spelling	_____ Spelling Challenge	_____ Spelling Challenge
Comprehension	_____ Books Read	_____ Books Read

Celebrate Success

I am proud of _____

I have done well in this part of *System 44* because _____

_____

Reflect

I am struggling with _____

This is challenging because _____

Teacher Comments: _____

_____

My Software Tracking Log

Place a sticker on the chart below each time you complete a topic. Use your Fast Track stickers when you fast track!

1	2	3	4	5	6	7	8	9	10	11	12	13
1.1	2.1	3.1	4.1	5.1	6.1	7.1	8.1	9.1	10.1	11.1	12.1	13.1
1.2	2.2	3.2	4.2	5.2	6.2	7.2	8.2	9.2	10.2	11.2	12.2	13.2
1.3	2.3	3.3	4.3	5.3	6.3	7.3	8.3	9.3	10.3	11.3	12.3	13.3
1.4	2.4	3.4	4.4	5.4	6.4	7.4	8.4	9.4	10.4	11.4	12.4	13.4
1.5	2.5	3.5	4.5	5.5	6.5	7.5	8.5	9.5	10.5	11.5	12.5	13.5
1.6	2.6	3.6	4.6	5.6	6.6	7.6	8.6	9.6	10.6	11.6	12.6	13.6
1.7	2.7	3.7				7.7	8.7		10.7	11.7		
1.8	2.8	3.8					8.8		10.8			

14	15	16	17	18	19	20	21	22	23	24	25
14.1	15.1	16.1	17.1	18.1	19.1	20.1	21.1	22.1	23.1	24.1	25.1
14.2	15.2	16.2	17.2	18.2	19.2	20.2	21.2	22.2	23.2	24.2	25.2
14.3	15.3	16.3	17.3	18.3	19.3	20.3	21.3	22.3	23.3	24.3	25.3
14.4	15.4	16.4	17.4	18.4	19.4	20.4	21.4	22.4	23.4	24.4	25.4
14.5	15.5	16.5	17.5	18.5	19.5	20.5	21.5	22.5	23.5	24.5	25.5
14.6			17.6		19.6	20.6	21.6			24.6	
14.7			17.7		19.7	20.7					

My Success Reads

Each time you read a Success passage, write down the date and the number of seconds it takes. Build your fluency.

Series	1st Read		2nd Read		3rd Read	
	Date	**Seconds**	**Date**	**Seconds**	**Date**	**Seconds**
1. *Bats Do That?* **Words:** 30						
2. *Art for Kicks* **Words:** 37						
3. *Run, Jesse, Run* **Words:** 58						
4. *Passing the Sniff Test* **Words:** 30						
5. *Brain Freeze* **Words:** 52						
6. *King of the Court* **Words:** 71						
7. *Something Fishy* **Words:** 44						
8. *High-Flying Circus* **Words:** 52						
9. *Struggle for Survival* **Words:** 56						
10. *Live From the Hive* **Words:** 85						
11. *Hero of Hope* **Words:** 79						
12. *Up and Running* **Words:** 93						
13. *Flies That Spy* **Words:** 76						

Series	1st Read		2nd Read		3rd Read	
	Date	**Seconds**	**Date**	**Seconds**	**Date**	**Seconds**
14. *Robots: Now It's Personal* **Words:** 63						
15. *Hail to the Chef* **Words:** 80						
16. *Going Coastal* **Words:** 88						
17. *The Dream Team* **Words:** 83						
18. *Get Ready to Roll!* **Words:** 81						
19. *Shark Attack?* **Words:** 83						
20. *A Born Winner* **Words:** 90						
21. *Get Down and Clown!* **Words:** 86						
22. *Pit Crew U* **Words:** 86						
23. *Look Out Below!* **Words:** 93						
24. *Back in Action* **Words:** 93						
25. *Congratulations!* **Words:** 99						

My Success Response Log

Keep track of the Success Series you have completed. Write the date that you finished the series. Then complete the sentence starter for each Success topic.

Series 1	**Bats Do That?**
	Date Completed: _____
	In *Bats Do That?*, I learned _____
	_____
	_____

Series 2	**Art for Kicks**
	Date Completed: _____
	Art for Kicks is about _____
	_____
	_____

Series 3	**Run, Jesse, Run**
	Date Completed: _____
	In *Run, Jesse, Run*, Jesse Owens _____
	_____
	_____

Series 4	**Passing the Sniff Test**
	Date Completed: _____
	Passing the Sniff Test is about dogs that _____
	_____
	_____

Series 5	*Brain Freeze*

Date Completed: _____

Brain scientists in *Brain Freeze* _____

_____

_____

Series 6	*King of the Court*

Date Completed: _____

In *King of the Court*, Pancho Gonzales _____

_____

_____

Series 7	*Something Fishy*

Date Completed: _____

Something Fishy is about _____

_____

_____

Series 8	*High-Flying Circus*

Date Completed: _____

The school in *High-Flying Circus* is special because _____

_____

_____

Series 9	***Struggle for Survival***

Date Completed: _____

Struggle for Survival is about _____

_____

_____

Series 10	***Live From the Hive***

Date Completed: _____

In *Live From the Hive*, I learned _____

_____

_____

Series 11	***Hero of Hope***

Date Completed: _____

In *Hero of Hope*, Emmanuel _____

_____

_____

Series 12	***Up and Running***

Date Completed: _____

Up and Running is about kids who _____

_____

_____

Series 13 — Flies That Spy

Date Completed: _____

In *Flies That Spy*, engineers are _____

_____

_____

Series 14 — Robots: Now It's Personal

Date Completed: _____

In *Robots: Now It's Personal*, Cynthia _____

_____

_____

Series 15 — Hail to the Chef

Date Completed: _____

Hail to the Chef is about _____

_____

_____

Series 16 — Going Coastal

Date Completed: _____

In *Going Coastal*, I learned _____

_____

_____

| Series 17 | **The Dream Team** |

Date Completed: _____

The Dream Team is about teens in Alaska who _____

_____

_____

| Series 18 | **Get Ready to Roll!** |

Date Completed: _____

Get Ready to Roll! is about _____

_____

_____

| Series 19 | **Shark Attack?** |

Date Completed: _____

In *Shark Attack?*, I discovered _____

_____

_____

| Series 20 | **A Born Winner** |

Date Completed: _____

In *A Born Winner*, Kyle _____

_____

_____

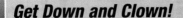

Series 21	**Get Down and Clown!**

Date Completed: _____

Get Down and Clown! is about _____

_____

Series 22	**Pit Crew U**

Date Completed: _____

Pit Crew U is a special school for _____

_____

Series 23	**Look Out Below!**

Date Completed: _____

In *Look Out Below!*, I learned _____

_____

Series 24	**Back in Action**

Date Completed: _____

In *Back in Action*, technology _____

_____

Series 25	**Congratulations!**

Date Completed: _____

For my future, I predict _____

_____

My Independent Reading Response Log

Book Title: _____

Phonics Focus: _____

S.M.A.R.T. WORDS   Date Completed: _____

Write each S.M.A.R.T. Word and rate it. Then, write a sentence that uses each word.

Word	Sentence
1. [1] [2] [3] [4]	
2. [1] [2] [3] [4]	
3. [1] [2] [3] [4]	
4. [1] [2] [3] [4]	
5. [1] [2] [3] [4]	

DURING READING   Date Completed: _____

Answer each question on the line below:

1. (page #_____) _____

_____

_____

2. (page #_____) _____

_____

_____

3. (page #_____) _____

_____

AFTER READING   Date Completed: _____

Use the sentence starters to write your answer to the questions.

1. _____

_____

_____

2. _____

_____

_____

                                            Date Completed: _____

Answer the reread question here:

_____

_____

_____

WRAP-UP

Rate this book by coloring in the number of stars:

☆ ☆ ☆ ☆ ☆

My *Reading Counts!* Quiz Score: _____

TEACHER FEEDBACK

                                            Date Completed: _____

My Independent Reading Response Log

Book Title: _____

Phonics Focus: _____

S.M.A.R.T. WORDS   Date Completed: _____

Write each S.M.A.R.T. Word and rate it. Then, write a sentence that uses each word.

Word	Sentence
1. 1 2 3 4	
2. 1 2 3 4	
3. 1 2 3 4	
4. 1 2 3 4	
5. 1 2 3 4	

DURING READING   Date Completed: _____

Answer each question on the line below:

1. (page #_____) _____

_____

_____

2. (page #_____) _____

_____

_____

3. (page #_____) _____

_____

AFTER READING

Date Completed: _____

Use the sentence starters to write your answer to the questions.

1. _____

_____

_____

2. _____

_____

_____

Date Completed: _____

Answer the reread question here:

_____

_____

_____

WRAP-UP

Rate this book by coloring in the number of stars:

☆ ☆ ☆ ☆ ☆

My *Reading Counts!* Quiz Score: _____

TEACHER FEEDBACK

Date Completed: _____

My Decodable Digest Response Log

Follow these steps to complete the Decodable Digest Routine.

1. Read the passage independently.
2. Reread the passage with your partner or group.
3. Record passage title, genre, and page number in the response log below.
4. In the log, record the targeted element from the green band at the top left. Then, record the pattern words.
5. Answer the React question and share your response.

Write your Decodable Digest titles and responses below.

Passage Title: _____   Genre: _____

Page Number: _____

Targeted Element: _____

Pattern Words:

1: _____   6: _____

2: _____   7: _____

3: _____   8: _____

4: _____   9: _____

5: _____   10: _____

React Question Response: _____

_____

_____

_____

_____

Passage Title: _____ Genre: _____

Page Number: _____

Targeted Element: _____

Pattern Words:

1: _____ 6: _____

2: _____ 7: _____

3: _____ 8: _____

4: _____ 9: _____

5: _____ 10: _____

React Question Response: _____

_____

_____

_____

_____

_____

_____

INDEPENDENT READING

Passage Title: _____ Genre: _____

Page Number: _____

Targeted Element: _____

Pattern Words:

1: _____ 6: _____

2: _____ 7: _____

3: _____ 8: _____

4: _____ 9: _____

5: _____ 10: _____

React Question Response: _____

_____

_____

_____

_____

_____

Passage Title: _____ Genre: _____

Page Number: _____

Targeted Element: _____

Pattern Words:

1: _____ 6: _____

2: _____ 7: _____

3: _____ 8: _____

4: _____ 9: _____

5: _____ 10: _____

React Question Response: _____

_____

_____

_____

_____

_____

_____

My *Phonics Inventory* Progress

Create a bar graph showing your *Phonics Inventory* fluency scores over the year. Set goals for improving your decoding status.

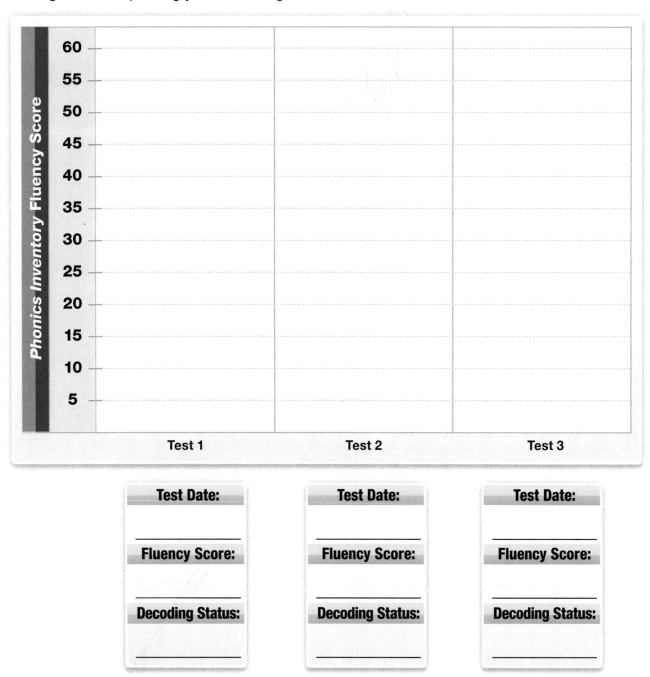

My *Reading Inventory* Progress

Create a bar graph showing your *Reading Inventory* Lexile® scores.
Set goals for improving your reading level.

Test Date:

_____

Test Score:

_____

Test Date:

_____

Test Score:

_____

Lexile Gain:

_____

My *Reading Counts!* Progress Chart

Write the title and date that you finished your book. Then enter your score for each *Reading Counts!* quiz. Fill in one box for every correct answer.

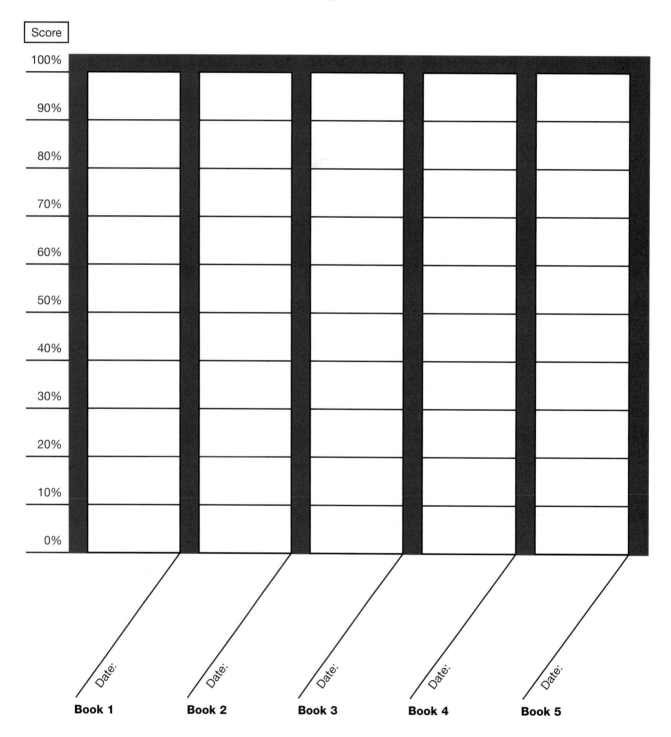

Score

100%
90%
80%
70%
60%
50%
40%
30%
20%
10%
0%

Date:
Date:
Date:
Date:
Date:

Book 1   **Book 2**   **Book 3**   **Book 4**   **Book 5**

My OFA Tracking Log

After your teacher checks your oral fluency, use this chart to track your Words Correct Per Minute (WCPM).

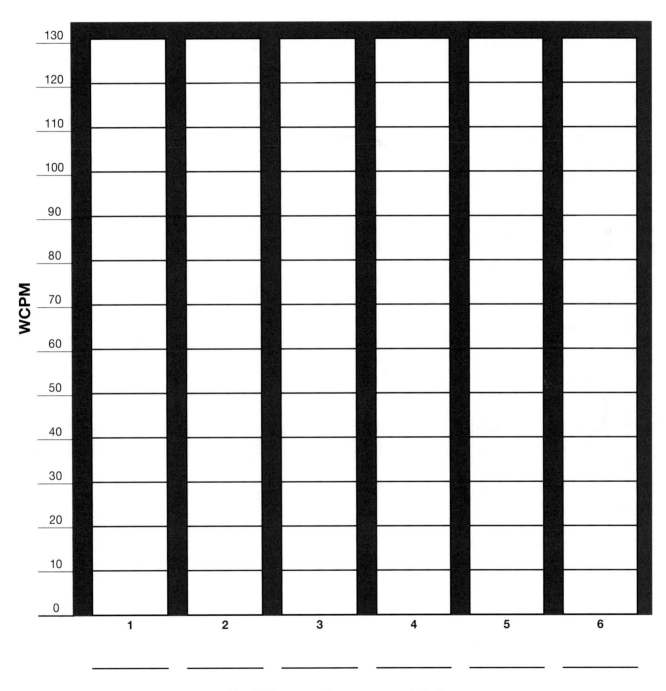

Oral Fluency Assessment Date

Small-Group Jobs

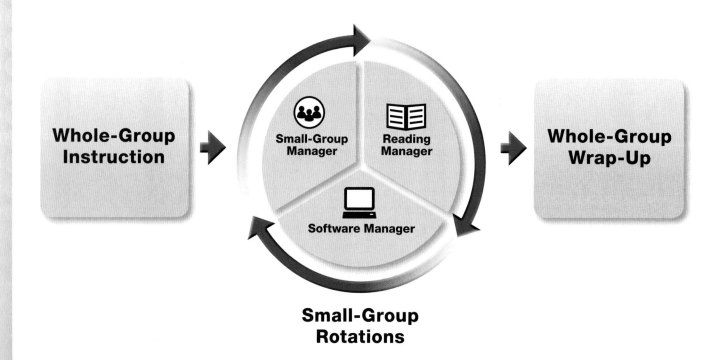

Reading Manager

1. Help your group members find their books.

2. Make sure everyone fills out the reading logs during the two-minute warning.

3. Make sure the reading area is organized before moving to the next rotation.

Group Name: _____

Student: _____

Group Name: _____

Student: _____

Group Name: _____

Student: _____

Software Manager

1. Help your group log on to the software.

2. If someone has a computer issue, help them troubleshoot. Restart the computer if necessary.

3. If you cannot help fix the computer issue, talk to the teacher.

4. Make sure the software area is organized before moving to the next rotation.

Group Name: _____

Student: _____

Group Name: _____

Student: _____

Group Name: _____

Student: _____

Small-Group Manager

1. Hand out all materials to each group member.

2. Partner with students who missed yesterday's lesson and help answer questions.

3. Make sure the small-group area is organized before moving to the next rotation.

Group Name: _____

Student: _____

Group Name: _____

Student: _____

Group Name: _____

Student: _____

Other Jobs

_____   _____

_____   _____

My New Vocabulary Log

Keep track of new words you come across in your reading. For each word, write the meaning and an example that uses the word. If you can, draw a picture that will help you remember what the word means.

NEW WORD	MEANING	EXAMPLE	PICTURE

My Dictation

Write the sounds, words, or sentences you hear.

Sounds

1: _____ 3: _____ 5: _____

2: _____ 4: _____ 6: _____

Words

1: _____ 4: _____ 7: _____

2: _____ 5: _____ 8: _____

3: _____ 6: _____ 9: _____

Sentences

1. _____

_____

2. _____

_____

3. _____

_____

4. _____

_____

5. _____

_____

Six Syllable Types

1 Closed Syllable

A closed syllable ends in a consonant. It usually has a short vowel sound.

   a. **hun • dred**

   b. **fan • tas • tic**

   c. **traf • fic**

2 Consonant + -le, -el, or -al

The consonant + -le, -el, or -al pattern usually forms its own syllable. You can split a word with the consonant + -le, -el, or -al pattern before the consonant to make it easier to read.

   a. **an • gle**

   b. **tun • nel**

   c. **sig • nal**

3 VCe Syllable

Syllables with the vowel-consonant-e pattern (VCe) have a long vowel sound. When you split a word with this pattern into syllables, keep the letters of the VCe pattern together.

   a. **on • line**

   b. **com • pute**

   c. **base • ment**

4 Open Syllable

An open syllable ends in a vowel. It usually has a long vowel sound.

   a. **ca • ble**

   b. **le • gal**

   c. **mu • sic**

5 Vowel Team Syllable

When you split a word with a vowel team, keep the letters of the vowel team in the same syllable.

   a. **con • tain**

   b. **rea • son**

   c. **dis • count**

   d. **free • dom**

6 r-Controlled Vowel Syllable

When the letter r follows a vowel, the r can change the sound the vowel stands for.

   a. **a • part • ment**

   b. **per • son**

   c. **re • turn**

   d. **thirst • y**

Word Attack Strategy

1 **Look**

2 **Spot**

3 **Split**

4 **Read**

Using the Strategy

Strategy Step	Examples	
1 **Look** for any prefixes, suffixes, or endings you know. • Remember, the spelling of the base word may have changed when the ending or suffix was added.	admitted admit(t) • <u>ed</u>	undefeated <u>un</u> • defeat • <u>ed</u>
2 **Spot** the vowels in the base word. The number of vowel spots tells the number of syllables. • Remember, some vowel sounds are spelled with more than one letter.	**a**dmit(t) • ed	un • d**efea**t • ed
3 **Split** the word into syllables. • A good place to split a word is between two consonants. • If there is only one consonant between syllables, try splitting after it. • If the word doesn't sound right, try moving the split backward or forward by one letter.	a<u>d</u> • <u>mi</u>t(t) • ed	~~un • def • eat • ed~~ un • d<u>e</u> • f<u>ea</u>t • ed
4 **Read** the word. Does it make a real word? If it does not, try again. • You may need to experiment with pronouncing the vowel sound differently.	admitted	undefeated

Affixes

Prefix

A word part added at the beginning of a base word to change its meaning.

Prefix	Meaning	Example
un-	not or opposite of	unlock
non-	not or opposite of	nonslip
de-	opposite of	defrost
com-	with	combine
con-	with	consist
re-	again	rewrite
pre-	before	pretest
mid-	in the middle of	midtown
sub-	below	subset
dis-	not or do the opposite of	disagree
mis-	badly or incorrectly	misspell
uni-	one	unicycle
bi-	two	bicycle
tri-	three	tricycle

Suffix

A word part added at the end of a base word to change its meaning or part of speech.

Suffix	Meaning	Example
-ment	state or condition	contentment
-ness	state or condition	stillness
-y	being, having, able to	lucky
-ly	like or in a _____ way	safely
-er	one who does something	teacher
-or	one who does something	actor
-er	compares two things or people	quicker
-est	compares more than two things or people	quickest
-less	without	spotless
-ful	causing or full of	cheerful
-tion	the state of	celebration
-sion	the state of	decision
-able	is or can be	adorable
-ible	is or can be	reversible

Root

Part of an English word that comes from other languages such as Latin or Greek.

Prefix	Meaning	Example
bio	life	biography
graph	something written or drawn	graphics
auto	self	autobiography
port	carry	portable
dict	to say	dictate
rupt	break	erupts

Prefix	Meaning	Example
struct	build	construct
scrib/ script	write	scribble
scope	to watch or look at	microscope
tele	far off	television
phon	sound or voice	telephone
vis/vid	to see	visible

Acknowledgments

Grateful acknowledgment is made to the following sources for permission to reprint from previously published material. The publisher has made diligent efforts to trace the ownership of all copyrighted material in this volume and believes that all necessary permissions have been secured. If any errors or omissions have inadvertently been made, proper corrections will gladly be made in future editions.

"Storm Survivor" adapted from "First Person: From Hurricane to Oil Spill" by Abigayle Lista from the Scholastic Teachers Website. Copyright © Scholastic Inc. All rights reserved.

"Epilogue" from *I Is a Long Memoried Woman* by Grace Nichols. Copyright © 1984 by Grace Nichols. Reprinted by permission of Curtis Brown London as agent for the author.

Adapted from "This Land Is My Land?" by Tasnim Mohamed. Copyright © Scholastic Inc. Reprinted by permission of the Alliance for Young Artists & Writers.

CREDITS

Credits

Cover (top to bottom): © Michael Appleton/NY Daily News Archive via Getty Images, © Dirk Eisermann/laif/Redux, © Gunnar Ask/AP Images, © Thinkstock, © Bettmann/Corbis, © Ben Curtis/AP Images, © John Mitchell/Photo Researchers, Inc., Jeff Rigby © Scholastic Inc., © Hemera/Thinkstock, Mike Lewis, Patsy Lynch/FEMA, © imago/Xinhua/Newscom, © ermess/Thinkstock; Backcover (top to bottom): © Thinkstock, © Dave Martin/AP Images, Tim Marrs © Scholastic Inc., © imago/Xinhua/Newscom, © Jochen Rolfes/plainpicture/Glow Images, Jeff Rigby © Scholastic Inc., © Mike Lewis, © Laurence Mouton/MediaBakery, © Samantha Mitchell/Image Source, © Ian Lishman/MediaBakery, © Bettmann/Corbis; p. 2 t (flag): © Thinkstock, t (girls): © MediaBakery, t (skyline): © Thinkstock, t (statue): © Thinkstock, b: © Dave Martin/AP Images; p. 3 t: Tim Marrs © Scholastic Inc., c: © imago/Xinhua/Newscom, b: © Jochen Rolfes/plainpicture/Glow Images; p. 4 t: Jeff Rigby © Scholastic Inc., c: © Mike Lewis, b: © Laurence Mouton/MediaBakery, b: © Samantha Mitchell/Image Source, b: © Ian Lishman/MediaBakery; p. 5 t: © Bettmann/Corbis; p. 6 tl (background): © Thinkstock, tl: © MediaBakery, tr: © Dave Martin/AP Images, bl: Tim Marrs © Scholastic Inc., br: © imago/Xinhua/Newscom; p. 7 tl: © Jochen Rolfes/plainpicture/Glow Images, tr: Jeff Rigby © Scholastic Inc., c: © Mike Lewis, bl: © Laurence Mouton/MediaBakery, br: © Bettmann/Corbis; p. 10 background: © Thinkstock, bl: © MediaBakery, b: © Thinkstock, br: © Thinkstock; p. 11 t: © Ben Curtis/AP Images, c: United States Government Printing Office, b: © Jeff Topping/Reuters; p. 12 l: © Adam Kazmierski/iStockphoto, r: © Image Source/Thinkstock; p. 13 tl: © Medioimages/Photodisc/Thinkstock, cl: © Pemotret/Dreamstime, bl: © David De Lossy/Thinkstock, tr: © iStockphoto/Thinkstock, cr: © iStockphoto/Thinkstock, br: © Image Source/Thinkstock; p. 14 t: © Ben Curtis/AP Images; p. 15 t: © Eliza Snow/iStockphoto, b: © Ana Abejon/iStockphoto; p. 16 l: United States Government Printing Office, c: United States Government Printing Office; p. 19 t: © Jeff Topping/Reuters; pp. 20–21: © Dave Martin/AP Images; p. 21 t: © Scholastic Inc., c: Satellite image by GeoEye, b: © Drew Perine /The News Tribune/AP Images; p. 22 l: © Comstock Images/Thinkstock, r: © Monkey Business/Fotolia; p. 24 t: © Mehmet Ali Cida/iStockphoto, t (tape): © loops7/iStockphoto, t (paperclip): © Koya79/Dreamstime, b: © Scholastic Inc.; p. 25 t: © Mari Darr-Welch/AP Images, t (tape): © loops7/iStockphoto; p. 26 c: © AP Images/Aerial imagery courtesy of MJ Harden, a GeoEye Company; pp. 26–27 background: © Afhunta/Dreamstime; p. 29 t: © The News Tribune, Drew Perine/AP Images; pp. 30–31: Tim Marrs © Scholastic Inc.; p. 31 t: © Mark Stay/iStockphoto, c: © Paula Nicho Cumez, b: Courtesy Tasnim Mohamed; p. 32 l: © Photos.com/Thinkstock, r: © Photodisc/Thinkstock, background: © fonikum/iStockphoto; pp. 34–35 background: © Hemera/Thinkstock; p. 35 t: © Mark Stay/iStockphoto; p. 36: © Paula Nicho Cumez; p. 38 c: Courtesy Tasnim Mohamed, bl: © Americanspirit/Dreamstime; pp. 38–39 t: © Swisshippo/Dreamstime; pp. 38–39 b: © Brandon Seidel/Dreamstime; pp. 40–41: © imago/Xinhua/Newscom; p. 41 t: © Gunnar Ask/AP Images, c: Robert Minor The Daily Worker via Harry Ransom Center, University of Texas at Austin, b: © John Van Hasselt/Sygma/Corbis; p. 42 t: © Martin Harvey/MediaBakery, b: © Anne Montfort/Glow Images; p. 44 tl: © Gunnar Ask/AP Images; p. 45 b: © Dirk Eisermann/laif/Redux; p. 46 c: Robert Minor The Daily Worker via Harry Ransom Center, University of Texas at Austin, t: © Picsfive/Dreamstime; pp. 46–47 background: © Iwona Rajszczak/iStockphoto; p. 48 t: © John Van Hasselt/Sygma/Corbis; p. 49 l: Courtesy Fair Trade USA, r: Courtesy GoodWeave; p. 51 l: © Florian Kopp/imagebroker/Newscom, r: © Dan White/Alamy; pp. 54–55: © Jochen Rolfes/plainpicture/Glow Images; p. 55 t: © John Dunn/AP Images, c: © Bettmann/Corbis, b: © Celluloid Dreams/Courtesy Everett Collection; p. 56 t: © Andy Gehrig/iStockphoto, c: © Ben Blankenburg/Corbis, b: © Matt Rourke/AP Images; p. 58 b: © John Dunn/AP Images; p. 60 c: © Bettmann/Corbis; pp. 60–61 background: © Ivan Ivanov/Thinkstock; p. 62 b: © Celluloid Dreams/Courtesy Everett Collection; p. 65 l: © Cleve Bryant/PhotoEdit, r: © Lynn Koenig/Getty Images; pp. 68–69: Jeff Rigby © Scholastic Inc.; p. 69 t: © Photomoephotos/Getty Images, c: © Paul Sharp, b: © Raul Allen © Scholastic Inc.; p. 72 c: © Photomoephotos/Getty Images; pp. 72–73 t: © ermess/Thinkstock; p. 73 tr: © ermess/Thinkstock; p. 74 l: © Paul Sharp, r: Library of Congress; pp. 74–75 background: © Yury Maselov/Thinkstock; pp. 76–77: © Raul Allen © Scholastic Inc.; p. 78 l: © Dominique Bertail, r: © Dominique Bertail; p. 82 background: © Mike Lewis; p. 83 t: The Valdosta Daily Times, c: Jack Newell Callahan, b: USDA Photo by R. Anson Eaglin; p. 86 t: The Valdosta Daily Times, b: © Greg Henry/iStockphoto; p. 88 c: Jack Newell Callahan; pp. 88–89 background: © Annieannie/Dreamstime; p. 91 t: USDA Photo by R. Anson Eaglin; p. 93 l: © Jason Edwards/National Geographic Stock, r: © John Mitchell/Photo Researchers, Inc.; p. 96 t: © Laurence Mouton/MediaBakery, c: © Samantha Mitchell/Image Source, b: © Ian Lishman/MediaBakery; p. 97 t: "Justice Mandala" Groundswell © 2011, b: © Webb Chappell, c: "Communidad Global, Global Community" Groundswell © 2011; p. 100 t: © Go Media, Inc.; pp. 100–101 b: © Manuel Gutjahr/iStockphoto; p. 101 c: "Justice Mandala" Groundswell © 2011, c (background): © Manuel Gutjahr/iStockphoto; p. 102 c: «Communidad Global, Global Community" Groundswell © 2011; pp. 102–103 background: © Olena Chernenko/iStockphoto; p. 104 c: © Webb Chappell; p. 107 l: © Chris Hyde/Getty Images, r: © Mark Bowden/iStockphoto; p. 110 background: © Bettmann/Corbis; p. 111 t: © Bettmann/Corbis, c: Library of Congress, b: © Michael Appleton/NY Daily News Archive via Getty Images; p. 114 b: © G. Paul Burnett/The New York Times, b (background): © Bettmann/Corbis; pp. 114–115 t: © Herbert Gehr/Time Life Pictures/Getty Images; p. 116 c: Library of Congress; pp. 116–117 background: © Thomas Pozzo Di Borgo/Dreamstime; p. 118 b: © Michael Appleton/NY Daily News Archive via Getty Images; p. 126 t: © Yuriy Zelenen'kyy/Dreamstime, c: © Amy Davis/Baltimore Sun/MCT via Getty Images, b: Library of Congress; p.127 t: © humonia/iStockphoto, c: © James King-Holmes/Science Source, b: © Time Life Pictures/Getty Images; p.128 t: © Vangert/Dreamstime, c: © Ann Heisenfelt/AP Images, b: © Torsten Krueger/Thinkstock; p. 129 t: © Zoonar/Thinkstock, b: © Daniel J. Barry/Getty Images; p.130 t: © Bob Daemmrich/Alamy, b: © Patrick Aventurier/GAMMA/Getty Images; p. 131 t: © Lisa Poole/AP Images, b: © Susan Walsh/AP Images; p. 132 t: © dblight/iStockphoto, b: © Marc Lester/AP Images; p. 133 t: © Philippa Banks/Thinkstock, b: © Fred Bavendam/Minden Pictures/Corbis; p. 134 t: © John Amis/AP Images, b: © DL1 WENN Photos/Newscom; p. 135 t: © Alan Ashley/SCG/ZUMA Press/Newscom, b: © Nicke Hallgren/iStockphoto; p. 136 t: © Waltraud Grubitzsch/EPA via Newscom; p. 137 t: © CJ Gunther/EPA/Newscom; p. 158 t: © Yuriy Zelenen'kyy/Dreamstime, c: © Amy Davis/Baltimore Sun/MCT via Getty Images, c: Library of Congress, b: © humonia/iStockphoto; p. 159 t: © James King-Holmes/Science Source, c: © Time Life Pictures/Getty Images, c: © Vangert/Dreamstime, b: © Ann Heisenfelt/AP Images; p. 160 t: © Torsten Krueger/Thinkstock, c: © Zoonar/Thinkstock, c: © Daniel J. Barry/Getty Images, b: © Bob Daemmrich/Alamy; p. 161 t: © Patrick Aventurier/GAMMA/Getty Images, c: © Lisa Poole/AP Images, c: © Susan Walsh/AP Images, b: © dblight/iStockphoto; p. 162 t: © Marc Lester/AP Images, c: © Philippa Banks/Thinkstock, c: © Fred Bavendam/Minden Pictures/Corbis, b: © John Amis/AP Images; p. 163 t: © DL1 WENN Photos/Newscom, c: © Alan Ashley/SCG/ZUMAPRESS/Newscom, c: © Nicke Hallgren/iStockphoto, b: © Waltraud Grubitzsch/EPA via Newscom, b: © CJ Gunther/EPA/Newscom; p. 184 tl: © Jeffrey Vock.